Dispelling the Myth
of Globalization

Dispelling the Myth of Globalization

The Case for Regionalization

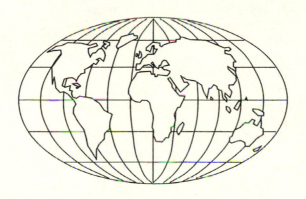

Hazel J. Johnson

PRAEGER

Westport, Connecticut
London

Library of Congress Cataloging-in-Publication Data

Johnson, Hazel.
    Dispelling the myth of globalization : the case for
      regionalization / Hazel J. Johnson.
      p.   cm.
    Includes bibliographical references and index.
    ISBN 0-275-93795-X (alk. paper)
    1. International economic integration. 2. Protectionism. 3. Free
trade. 4. International economic relations. I. Title.
HF1418.5.J65   1991
337–dc20   91-4281

British Library Cataloguing in Publication Data is available.

Library of Congress Catalog Card Number: 91-4281
ISBN: 0-275-93795-X

First published in 1991

Praeger Publishers, 88 Post Road West, Westport, CT 06881
An imprint of Greenwood Publishing Group, Inc.

Printed in the United States of America

The paper used in this book complies with the
Permanent Paper Standard issued by the National
Information Standards Organization (Z39.48–1984).

10 9 8 7 6 5 4 3 2

"This little light of mine, let it shine, let it shine."

In Loving Memory of My Mother,
Ida Wilma Kelly

Contents

Tables

Preface

The notion of global markets for goods and services is appealing. Communications, travel, and trade are now less restricted by national borders than at any time in the past. However, closer examination of the flow of capital, trade relationships, and income levels reveals strong regional patterns of development. Thus, *regionalization* frequently appears to be a better description of world market evolution than globalization.

During the 1980s in the United States, disturbing trends began to develop. Severe trade and budget imbalances contributed to the first decline in living standards in decades. Further south in the Western Hemisphere, the countries of Latin America suffered from declining economic activity and mounting external debt. This volatile mix of circumstances threatens the long-term economic health of the United States. There appears to be a migration toward the United States from Latin America as conditions there become increasingly intolerable. The low-cost labor pool just south of the border already has attracted many manufacturing jobs that once were held by U.S. citizens. Unless conditions are stabilized in Latin America, recent trends probably will accelerate.

Further, it is unlikely that the rest of the industrialized world will help rectify these problems, unless the United States actively promotes a comprehensive plan to bolster the Latin American economies. While to initiate a nontraditional scheme to assist Latin America may be above and beyond the call of duty, not to do so is to almost certainly guarantee an unbearable immigration

problem and severe financial and economic distress in the United
States.

Beyond the Western Hemisphere, a realistic assessment of other
regions provides little, if any, evidence of global development. Today's
Japanese economic policy is all too reminiscent of its former military
policy. Post–World War II economic strategies have brought corporate
dominance to Japan that is not at all unlike that which occurred during
the days of the samurais. Essentially, in Japan, *government policy is
industrial policy*. The role for other countries of the world falls into one
of three categories. A foreign country can be an export market for
Japanese goods, a learning lab from which to cultivate their own
technological advances, or a cheap labor pool. As the Japanese say one
thing and consistently do another, it appears that Asia is being built as
a Japanese economic empire of former colonies, Europe is shaping up as
the next major export market for Japan, and the burden of Latin America
will fall on the shoulders of the United States.

Outside Japan, the rest of Asia has been spurred to rates of economic
growth unparalleled in any other region. Given the amount of money
that has been invested in this area, such results should not really
be surprising. In determining whether the direction of these capital
flows is reflective of globalization or regionalization, it is interesting
to note that the Asian phenomenon occurred at the same time that
Japan was building up huge trade surpluses. If economic trends are truly
global, why did Asia benefit more than Latin America or Sub-Saharan
Africa?

Nevertheless, storm clouds are brewing in this dynamic region. The
1997 Chinese takeover of Hong Kong has many investors worried. In
this climate of uncertainty about Hong Kong's future autonomy,
Singapore probably will rise to even greater stature in world financial
and industrial circles. However, past activism on the mainland will not
be subdued forever, even with the central government attempting to
recentralize the country. The proverbial horse is out of the barn. It will
do no good to close the door at this point. To accommodate this
irreversible tide of decentralization, democracy, and free enterprise,
Beijing may find Taiwan to be a useful tool of capitalism. To date, the
People's Republic of China (PRC) has had some difficulty attracting
the kind of foreign investment that it seeks, that is, export-oriented,
high-tech industries — on its own terms. Usurping Taiwanese capital
and expertise may enable the central planners to accomplish its
agenda. Of course, at this point, the Nationalists of Taiwan are just as
likely to view the chaos that almost certainly will erupt on the
mainland as an opportunity to take control of Beijing once again.

Meanwhile, the often-discussed reunification of North and South Korea will be infinitely more difficult than its German counterpart. There is neither the industrial capacity nor the export potential for a unified Korea that would be adequate to smoothly absorb the Communists. Korea probably will be forced to turn to Japan for help and, in that event, Japan will exact concessions from Korea. These concessions may, indeed, be similar to those of the days of Japanese occupation. In all, the 1990s promise to be turbulent for the entire region as it grapples with its newly found affluence and social change.

In Europe, the Single European Market holds much promise of a unified region with economic power that could potentially outpace the United States of America. Yet, the past hostilities of these countries do not really suggest one dominant nation even though Germany is often cast in this role. The real surprise may be the growth of the United Kingdom as it capitalizes on its restructuring of the 1980s and learns lessons of development from former and soon-to-be-former colonies of Singapore and Hong Kong. Export industries and international financial services are the critical factors for the United Kingdom. On the other hand, the now powerful Germany will find that it has bitten off more than it can chew with its recent reunification. The cost of restructuring and rebuilding the former East Germany is already high and probably will continue to mount as more realistic estimates of the total bill emerge. The rest of the former Soviet satellites also may see Germany as the answer to their collective problems of antiquated industrial infrastructure, lack of consumer goods, and limited understanding of capitalist systems. In attempting to meet these expectations, Germany may be forced to consider countertrade with underdeveloped countries outside Europe in order to relieve the problems of unemployment and slumping industrial output. In this regard, Sub-Saharan Africa offers some promise.

For its part, the Soviet Union has managed to create in Eastern Europe one of the worst tragedies of human development in recorded history and is now, essentially, walking away and leaving the problems to industrialized countries of the West. Caught in the middle, of course, are the former satellites. They are neither Sovietlike nor Westernized. Under these circumstances, it is not inconceivable that several of them could form a neutral trading block and capitalize on their individual strengths in the transition to modern economies. Members of this block could include Yugoslavia (already a neutral country), Hungary, and Czechoslovakia. Poland, too, may join. In fact, Germany may underwrite Poland in this effort, thus creating a neutral buffer between it and the Soviet Union.

While the world is fascinated by the tremendous growth of Asia and by the rapid change in Eastern Europe, the poorest region of the world struggles to survive. Sub-Saharan Africa is a paradox in that 30 of the world's 50 poorest countries are located there but that the abundance of natural resources in the region is unparalleled. One of the primary problems is that former European masters did little to transfer technology upon their departure. This is further complicated by Arab neighbors that seem more intent on enslaving the region than on mutual development. One reasonable approach to correct this situation is for Sub-Saharan Africans to work with African descendants in other countries to promote activities to their mutual benefit.

The United States has some restructuring of its own to do if it is to avoid further declines in its standard of living. Small firms are the key to these changes on the industrial front. In the declining cities, more realistic policies will be required to reverse the outflow of people and capital. In fact, new experimental cities are needed to take advantage of the technology that is already available but underutilized. In short, more innovation in the United States must be forthcoming. The days of world supremacy for the United States are now history. They can only be revisited if Americans view the world as it really is — a regionalized configuration of countries breaking with the past and embracing the future in the pursuit of their own agendas. Perhaps, the United States should do the same.

Is not U.b.
win - win
us enslvmt

1
Globalization or Regionalization?

THE MEANING OF GLOBALIZATION

"World global markets" is a catchy phrase that has become all too common in discussions of current and future economic development. It is a tempting concept that conjures up images of communications and exchanges of goods and services without regard to national boundaries. In fact, "globalization" of information flows is a reasonable characterization. Advanced telecommunications have made it possible for ideas and images to be transmitted almost instantaneously throughout the world. In addition, many large U.S. firms find overseas markets to be the most fertile ground for future growth. Clearly, just as many foreign firms have found the U.S. market to be a gold mine in terms of distribution of their own products. These forms of activity encourage acceptance of the concept of globalization of world markets. *, true libr/sm

However, what is less well understood is that true globalization means that there should be roughly uniform capital flows into all developing regions, that is, that regions should attract investments in accordance with the competitive advantages that they hold. In a truly global economy, there should be no pockets of stagnant growth where disciplined work forces and/or abundant natural resources are underutilized.

If some areas appear to receive more economic attention than others that are similarly endowed, then world markets are not global. This, in fact, is the case. *Regionalization* is a strong force that has and will continue to effect standards of living throughout the world. Regionalization will shift the balance of economic power away from the United States and toward Europe and Asia. The process has already begun and it will gain momentum, dragging down average U.S. incomes even further. Conditions in Latin America will deteriorate to such an extent that the United States will be faced with an ever-increasing immigration problem for which it has no viable corrective plan. The only way to avoid these outcomes is to recognize the phenomena and to accept the implications that they hold for American economic policy.

LATIN AMERICA: A TICKING BOMB

Conditions in Latin America have perhaps never been more volatile than they are at this point. Thousands of Argentines stand in line daily for government food handouts. Even so, half of all Argentine children under the age of two years are anemic because of inadequate nutrition. A total of 25 million citizens (78 percent of the total population struggle to survive on a family income of less than $100 per month. In Brazil, the world's eighth largest economy, many of the poor of Rio de Janeiro work as domestic servants to the rich but live in hillside slums warmed by leaking kerosene stoves. Respiratory disease and leprosy are treated by the only medical facility that has been established by a U.S. foundation.

Throughout Latin America, the gap between the rich and the poor is wide and widening. From 60 percent to 80 percent of all families are starving. The richest families earn a disproportionate share of total income.[1] Average income in South and Central America is a fraction of that in the United States and other developed countries.[2] Contributing to these problems are persistent debt-servicing difficulties. With 11 percent of the total population of developing countries, Latin America and the Caribbean owe 37 percent of developing country debt.[3] The burden of debt has contributed to an already dismal economic picture, resulting in inflation rates in the late 1980s that were reminiscent of those in Germany during the 1920s.[4]

Nor are Latin Americans calmly accepting these circumstances. Food riots and labor unrest are all too common. When the inflation rate reached 3,500 percent in Argentina, looters raided stores to steal food that they could no longer afford to buy. Organized labor in sectors ranging from bus drivers to metalworkers staged work slowdowns or threatened to do so. Variations on this theme have been repeated throughout the region.

New government administrations in the late 1980s and early 1990 attempted to introduce measures to curb inflation and restore monetary

#102   2012-03-14 7:18PM
Item(s) checked out to p13035745.

TITLE: Dispelling the myth of globalizat
BARCODE: 39345010788440
DUE DATE: 12-05-11

TITLE: Globalization and regionalization
CODE: 39345014332849
TE: 12-05-11

lization

order. However, whether the measures will be sufficient to permanently reverse recent economic trends is not at all clear. There appears to be no traditional way in which the region's external debt can be repaid or restructured. Complete debt relief for a minimum of 20 years will be required to allow Latin America to "grow" out of its predicament. A swap of 20-year zero-coupon bonds at market interest rates could provide the needed time. To render the bonds readily marketable, principal should be guaranteed by a consortium of industrialized countries that also oversees development efforts for the term during which the bonds are outstanding.

If it leads such a rescue of Latin America, the United States government will accomplish two vital objectives. First, it will help save its own banking system from what is now clearly the error of its ways during the 1970s and 1980s. In so doing, the pressure from both nonperforming domestic real estate and foreign loans can be partially alleviated, averting a repeat performance of the savings and loan fiasco.

Second, and equally important, a move to resolve the Latin American debt crisis and bring vitality back to the region will stop the migration of millions of Latin Americans that are slowly, but surely, migrating toward the United States. During the 1980s, the pattern of population growth leads one to no other conclusion than that the southern borders of the United States will eventually be overrun by people who are desperate to escape what seems to be an inevitable fate of long-term deprivation.

THE BUILDUP OF POPULATION NEAR U.S. BORDERS

From 1980 through 1990, the population of Central America alone increased by more than that of the entire United States.[5] In 1980, this region covered approximately one quarter of the land mass of the United States and its population stood at 41 percent of that of the United States. During the 1980s, the United States grew by 22.6 million residents (10 percent), Central America by 23.4 million (25 percent). Every newborn in the United States or immigrant to the United States had a counterpart just south of the border. On the other hand, growth in the U.S. population outpaced Canadian growth by a ratio of over 9 to 1.[6]

Interestingly, this high rate of population growth is not consistently observed throughout Latin America. In Chile, Argentina, Paraguay, and Uruguay, countries more removed from the United States, population increases were roughly proportional to those in the

United States.[7] Also, in several of the larger island nations, the rate of increase was more in line with that of the United States.[8] It is, perhaps, harder to migrate to the United States from so far south or over so much water.

A notable exception to the more moderate growth in the islands was the Dominican Republic. Here the population swelled by almost 30 percent. However, this, too, appears consistent with buildup near the southern borders since the Dominican Republic is separated from Puerto Rico by less than 100 miles of water. Once the perilous crossing has been accomplished, it is possible for an illegal immigrant to represent himself as a Puerto Rican and to board an airplane to New York City without presenting a passport. Thus, Puerto Rico is a gateway to the United States and the Dominican Republic is a gateway to Puerto Rico.

Further, the immigration buildup does not appear to be limited to Central America. In the northern region of South America, the 67 million residents of Columbia, Venezuela, Ecuador, and Peru constituted less than 30 percent of the total U.S. residents in 1980. However, during the next decade, the additional 18.5 million people in these four countries alone nearly matched U.S. growth (of 22.6 million) one-for-one. Collectively, the population increases of these four nations and Central America outpaced the United States by a factor of almost two-to-one.

What U.S. policymakers appear not to understand is that Latin American birth rates do not satisfactorily explain these patterns. The greatest population increases are observed in those regions that are closest to the United States, or as in the case of the Dominican Republic, have a viable gateway to the United States. Migration toward the United States should most certainly be considered a factor in observed differential growth rates. Considering the economic stress under which most Latin Americans must live, such migration is not at all irrational.

Clearly, the journey from Central America and adjacent countries is not particularly difficult, requiring only ground transportation. In fact, in many cases, it may appear preferable to walk, if need be, toward U.S. borders rather than to remain in countries that offer so little hope for survival.

This migration has profound implications for the United States. One can theorize that the rate of population growth for the entire region is a good proxy for the expected growth for any group of countries and that any excess over this amount could be related to the migration phenomenon. That is, if it is reasonable to assume that each country should have grown by the average growth rate for all Latin American countries, then growth beyond this may be associated with regional migration trends.

Such an exercise suggests that at least 6.7 million people in Central America and adjacent countries could be headed for the United States.[9] This would constitute almost 150 percent of all Latin American immigrants to the United States during the 26 years ended 1987.[10] This estimate is also roughly equivalent to the combined populations of Los Angeles, Miami, Fort Lauderdale, and Chicago.[11] Of course, it is possible that even this estimate is understated. However, the pressure that such a population shift would exert on U.S. employment, housing, and social services cannot be overstated. Unless conditions change such that there are fewer incentives for mass immigration, the influx will be unavoidable.

ECONOMIC NEGLECT OF LATIN AMERICA

How could conditions deteriorate to this degree right in the United States' own backyard? Was it a fluke or just "bad luck"? Regrettably, the conditions in Latin America are not coincidental. They are the result of economic neglect and of the failure of the United States to recognize that the standard of living of North Americans eventually would be affected by the standard of living of Central and South Americans.

The United States has not always been faced with this dilemma because Latin America has not always suffered from such an erosion of economic conditions. In fact, in the 1960s and 1970s, economies to the south grew and the future was bright. From 1965 through 1980, gross domestic investment and manufacturing output grew at average annual rates of 8.3 percent and 6.9 percent, respectively.[12]

Then the effects of oil shocks during the 1970s and attendant borrowing that was necessary to cover energy-related trade deficits became all too apparent. Between 1980 and 1987, gross domestic investment declined 4.5 percent each year, and manufacturing output increased at the low average rate of 0.6 percent. Meanwhile, domestic investment in East Asian developing countries expanded at the rate of 12 percent a year, boosting manufacturing output at an annual rate of 10.4 percent. No developing region can sustain economic growth and development when investment and output suffer the slow or negative growth that has been observed in Latin America in recent years.

Financial markets in developing countries are not always well developed enough to assure needed capital infusions from stock issuances or other forms of equity investment. Thus, there is frequently a strong dependence on forms of debt financing. In the latter half of the 1980s, no other region in the developing world sustained as much disinvestment as Latin America. From 1985 through 1989, Asian countries acquired a total of $49 billion through new international commercial bank loans and bond issues. New European financing was a distant second at $7 billion. However, the net changes in Latin America and Africa were reductions of $7 billion and $1.5 billion, respectively. For these latter two regions, the negative financial flows represented a significant departure from the experience of the early 1980s.[13]

Table 1.1 shows the effects of disinvestment on exports and gross national product (GNP).[14] During the 1970s, the strength of Latin American economies compared favorably with other developing regions. Exports and GNP grew at nominal annual rates of 21 percent and 16 percent, respectively. Latin American GNP actually grew faster than Asian. However, from 1980 through 1988, export growth was barely above 1 percent and GNP growth under 3 percent. Further, these percentages have not been adjusted for inflation. Doing so would yield negative growth rates for the period. However, those regions that received healthy doses of foreign capital fared much better. Table 1.1 clearly illustrates that there are, indeed, strong patterns of regional development, not one uniform global trend.

In addition to burdensome debt and inadequate domestic investment, another real problem for Latin America is that the United States has not fulfilled the role of an economic locomotive in the Western Hemisphere as Japan and Germany have in their respective regions. In fact, the United States actually has been an economic drain.

From 1980 through 1987, Japan and Germany accumulated trade surpluses of $608 billion. These surpluses made it possible for the two

TABLE 1.1
Regional Comparisons of Export and Income Growth,
1970–1980 and 1980–1988

| | Average Annual % Change | | | |
| | 1970-1980 | | 1980-1988 | |
	Exports	GNP	Exports	GNP
Latin America and the Caribbean	21.0%	16.4%	1.2%	2.9%
East Asia and the Pacific	26.3	15.0	8.5	4.7
South Asia	10.9	11.5	4.7	5.4
Europe and the Mediterranean	24.0	21.8	4.6	2.7
Sub-Saharan Africa	20.9	17.1	-4.8	-4.3
North Africa and the Middle East	26.4	17.8	-0.7	3.3

Source: Author's calculations based on data from World Bank. *World Debt Tables 1989–90: External Debt of Developing Countries*, vol. 1.

countries to reinvest within their regions, thereby stimulating neighboring economies. Over the same period, net short-term and long-term capital flows from Germany to other countries totaled $102 billion. For Japan, the total was $606 billion. In other words, over $700 billion was made available for investment purposes by these two countries alone, much of it because of trade surpluses.

However, from 1980 through 1987, the United States sustained trade deficits totaling $696 billion, making it necessary to import capital in the amount of $296 billion. Thus, instead of the United States making net investments in Latin America and elsewhere, it actually pulled almost $300 billion out of the pool of world capital. Sadly, the inflow of money appears to have had little impact on the country's worldwide competitiveness. Trade and fiscal deficits show no signs of reversing, average wages are falling, and foreign competitors within the U.S. market continue to gain market share.

By contrast, all of Latin America and the Caribbean attracted only $143 billion in short-term and long-term capital between 1980 and 1987.[15] However, net interest payments on external debt were well in excess of $200 billion. Thus the region is caught in a financial vice in which capital inflows are more than offset by required interest payments on old debt.

THE REALITIES OF LATIN AMERICAN DEBT

At the rate with which Latin American debt currently is being repaid, the region will only continue to be more indebted and real economic development will become even less feasible. Organizations such as the International Monetary Fund (IMF) and the World Bank have attempted to coordinate restructurings to relieve debt-servicing burdens and to, at least partially, satisfy lenders. This process typically involves deferring payments and/or reducing interest rates. The notion of debt forgiveness also has been incorporated recently. In exchange for these concessions, debtor nations agree to austerity programs, including, but not limited to, reductions in imports, reduced government spending, and constriction of domestic money supply to fight inflation.

Currently, the "menu" approach is being pursued. One of the most widely publicized of these has been orchestrated by U.S. Treasury Secretary Nicholas Brady — the "Brady Plan" — in the case of Mexico. According to the Brady Plan, commercial banks had several options from which to choose. One option was for banks to accept only 65 percent of the current loan balance in the form of Mexican government zero-coupon bonds. From the banks' perspective, the attractive feature of this option was that the 65 percent was collateralized by U.S. Treasury securities. The less attractive feature was that 35 percent of the loan balance was to be written off.

The second option also involved bond issuance, collateralized by Mexican bonds. However, in this case, full loan value would be exchanged for interest-bearing bonds. The less appealing provision was that these bonds would carry an interest rate of only two-thirds the market rate.

The last option was for new loans to Mexico for up to 25 percent of bank holdings of Mexican government bonds. Drafters of the plan no doubt anticipated that this third option would generate needed investment funds for the country. However, banks' response to this option was least enthusiastic, reflecting their collective reluctance to come forward with new money, which amounted to only $1.6 billion.

Nor did the response to the other two options eliminate Mexican debt to commercial banks. Less than half of Mexico's $84 billion private debt was affected by the Brady Plan. Loans of $19.6 billion (25 percent) were restructured to give the country complete debt relief for a substantial period of time, that is, converted into 30-year zero-coupon bonds after a 35 percent debt forgiveness. However, U.S. Treasury securities of $7 billion were purchased to back the bonds.

In addition, interest-bearing bonds with below-market rates were issued to replace $22.5 billion in loans on a dollar-for-dollar basis. Here too, $7 billion in U.S. securities had to be purchased.

Essentially, Mexico paid $14 billion to receive long-term debt relief on $19.6 billion in loans. In a sense, it is fortunate that no more bank debt was rescheduled because Mexico might have found itself in the position of not being able to afford any further debt restructuring. The legitimate question arises as to whether these exercises really benefit the developing countries for which they are intended.

Another legitimate question is whether the debt can ever be repaid. With only marginal reductions in cash outflows each year, so many resources continue to be devoted to debt service that significant economic growth appears highly unlikely. During the 1980s Latin American and Caribbean countries made total debt-servicing payments (interest and principal) of $518 billion. Yet, total debt outstanding almost doubled.[16]

Ideally, debt-servicing payments should be covered by a country's foreign exchange earnings on international trade, in other words, from export earnings. During the same ten-year period, aggregate regional trade surpluses (exports less imports) totaled $188 billion. In addition, new debt potentially added another $191 billion in liquidity. Combined, these trade and financial flows provided only $379 billion. Since debt-servicing payments of $518 billion exceeded this total, $139 billion was effectively wrung out of the consumption and investment activities of the region. In other words, consumers tightened their belts even further and desperately needed investments were foregone.

Clearly, debt-service relief must be instituted if Latin America is to have any chance for future development. Yet even in the face of these sobering realities, the response to debt reduction has been lukewarm on the part of creditors. A significant reason appears to be that the plans to date have all been piecemeal solutions, addressing a relatively small part of total debt for one country at a time. From the perspective of bankers, there is some incentive to "free ride," that is, to not participate in debt restructuring and forgiveness in anticipation of being one of the last banks with which the country negotiates. The rationale is that, at that point, the debtor nation may be more willing and able to pay off what remains of commercial bank debt. More charitably, there also may be some reluctance to set a precedent for other countries in which the bank may have some exposure. At any rate, a third question would appear to be whether the one-country-at-a-time approach can be effective.

The realities of the Latin American debt crisis suggest that the answers to all three questions are negative. The process is not helping investment-starved debtor nations. At this rate, the debt will never be repaid. Lastly, there is relatively little incentive for commercial banks to participate.

WHAT LATIN AMERICAN DEBT
MEANS TO THE UNITED STATES

The United States has a much greater stake in the resolution of Latin American debt than other industrialized countries. As noted above, it is the United States that will be hit with mass immigration if conditions do not improve in Latin America. In addition, it is U.S. banks that are most invested in these loans. U.S. bank exposure to Latin American debt was approximately $64 billion at the end of 1988 and was concentrated primarily in the country's larger banks.

As of that date, the cushion against loan loss for the large banks in New York, California, and Illinois totaled $75 billion.[17] This amount implied a capital ratio of 7.7 percent.[18] As of that date, if all Latin American loans were recognized as uncollectible and written off, this ratio would drop to 1.1 percent, the lowest in all industrialized countries.

Currently, such write-offs would only add to the not insignificant concern over excess bank exposure to real estate loans and the $500 billion bailout of the savings and loan industry. Under these circumstances, mass financial hysteria could easily lead to deposit withdrawals that would precipitate the collapse of the U.S. banking system.

The Latin American debt crisis cannot be ignored indefinitely. Strong leadership is needed to address the real problems in that region. Further, the United States has the most to lose should the worst case materialize and the most to gain should the situation be satisfactorily resolved.

A COMPREHENSIVE APPROACH TO RESOLUTION

To arrive at a reasonable solution, it is necessary to appreciate the positions of both commercial banks and Latin American debtor nations. U.S. commercial banks will be hard pressed to accept substantial write-offs. Developing debtor nations cannot continue to spend more on debt service than on capital investments.

A market-oriented, 20-year zero-coupon bond issue to replace the full value of outstanding debt, together with an additional $200 billion in new investment, will accommodate both parties. Such a bond issue would total $634 billion, with $434 billion in bonds replacing current outstanding debt. Full attention and effort could then be devoted to economic development rather than endless debt renegotiations. The $200 billion investment fund would breathe fresh air into the stagnant economic climate.

With respect to the specific attributes of the bond issue, it must be made attractive to the general investment community worldwide. An important consideration is the *risk profile* of the issue. To render credibility, the original investment ($634 billion) should be guaranteed by an international consortium of 20 high-income countries, including the United States, Japan, and Germany. It is noteworthy that this guarantee requires no cash outlay on the part of the members of the consortium and that the present value of the guarantee is substantially less than $634 billion. Assuming average 5 percent inflation over the 20-year period, the present value of this amount is $239 billion, or an average of $12 billion per consortium member.[19]

With this backing, the *interest rate* can be lower than it might be otherwise. Since Latin American countries vary in terms of their respective risk levels, the interest rate attached to the bonds should reflect this, as well as the safety feature of a guarantee. An assessment of the appropriate rate for each country can be weighted by that country's share of total debt outstanding at the time of bond issuance and this weighted average then adjusted downward in recognition of consortium participation. In other words, the interest rate would be a composite rate relevant for all bonds.

Making the issue *tax-exempt* will add a decidedly attractive feature. This would eliminate the need for investors to pay tax on the accrued interest each year, as is frequently the case with other zero-coupon bonds.

Marketability can be further enhanced if the consortium members act as *market makers.* It is not uncommon for the underwriter of a municipal bond issue to perform this function, standing ready to buy or sell the bonds to maintain an orderly market. At the international level, central banks commonly intervene in currency markets to assure order. Performing the same function for these bonds can assure large and small investors of liquidity.

In order to ensure that proper development measures are taken while Latin American countries are free of debt service, the consortium should also oversee *investment activities.* In fact, each country must agree to be advised by consortium representatives as a condition for participation in the plan. This conditionality assures two important outcomes. First, sharing the expertise of nations that are already economically strong can only enhance the development process. Secondly, investors will have more confidence that issuing countries will, indeed, emerge from this 20-year period financially stronger than when they entered.

From the perspective of existing creditors, the options are to hold new bonds, to receive a full-value cash payoff, or some combination of the two. Clearly, a guaranteed original investment (equal to the face value of current loans), an attractive interest rate, a strong secondary market in which to trade the bonds, and world-class technical assistance in the execution of industrial projects might be a combination that appeals to more than a few lenders. Should the current creditors decide to hold the bonds instead of "cashing out," issuers would then need to raise only the $200 billion necessary to establish the investment fund.

Nevertheless, in the minds of some potential investors there may remain two fundamental questions. Can capital markets absorb this volume of new financing? If the bonds are sold, what quantitative assurance is there that Latin American countries will be better able to handle the debt levels implied at the time of maturity?

The answer to the first question appears to be affirmative. International bond markets are currently expanding at an impressive rate. In 1982 $76 billion in international bonds were issued. By 1989 new issues for the year totaled $254 billion. This implies an average annual rate of growth of 19 percent. At this rate, the markets will be able to absorb over $600 billion by the year 1995. As noted above, if current lenders accept the consortium-underwritten bonds, it would be necessary to raise only $200 billion in cash sales.

The answer to the second question appears to be generally positive. Latin American countries should most certainly enjoy a better debt-to-income ratio as a result of this initiative. In 1989, external debt for the region totaled $434 billion, while aggregate GNP was $852 billion. Thus, debt to GNP was 51 percent. However, if all debt payments are deferred for 20 years and $200 billion is injected into the economies, it appears reasonable that the region could resume growth at rates comparable to those of the 1970s, when debt-service payments of $140 billion were made.

Assuming GNP grew at the average rate observed during the 1970s, that is, 16.4 percent in nominal terms (see Table 1.1), and the interest rate assigned to new bonds was 11 percent, debt to GNP would be significantly reduced to a more manageable 29 percent at the end of the 20-year period.[20] In the process, Latin America would become a stronger neighbor and trading partner for the United States. Equally important, a source of major instability in the Western Hemisphere would have been eliminated.

ACCEPTING THE IMPLICATIONS
OF REGIONALIZATION

Policymakers in the United States may have some reluctance to undertake such a comprehensive Latin American debt resolution, preferring to concentrate on domestic issues and the perhaps more fascinating process of democratization of Eastern Europe. However, at some point, developments in the southern portion of the Western Hemisphere will become more compelling than the momentous collapse of the Berlin Wall. At that point, there will be little, if any, assistance from other high-income nations. It is better to accept the inevitability of regional development while it is still possible to prevent the situation in the Western Hemisphere from degenerating into economic and financial chaos.

From a foreign policy standpoint, this also means viewing the rest of the world realistically, rather than idealistically. On both fronts, the United States must look beyond the surface and attempt to analyze regional developments with an appreciation for history and any cultural differences that may be relevant to its future relationships with the rest of the world.

The Japanese are truly intent on building a new empire, based in Asia, with affiliate offices around the world. Germany will find that it is committed to a reconstruction process in Eastern Europe that may well involve it in the economic fight of its life as it pursues a similar regional dominance. The Soviet Union is all too anxious to walk away from its past mistakes in Eastern Europe and let the industrialized West reward it for "doing the right thing." Meanwhile, foregone opportunities in resource-rich Sub-Saharan Africa are ignored.

In the United States, these developments suggest that business as usual will not be good enough. Without a healthy dose of American perestroika, it is possible that the United States will find itself — indeed, the entire Western Hemisphere — continuing to lose economic ground to those parts of the world that better understand the concept of regionalization.

NOTES

1. For example, in Argentina, Mexico, Chile, and Brazil, the richest 20 percent earned 50 percent, 58 percent, 60 percent, and 67 percent, respectively, of total 1988 family income. In the United States and Japan, the corresponding percentages were 40 percent and 38 percent, respectively (Ungeheuer, 1989).

2. Below are selected comparative per capita GNPs for 1988 (Source: *World Bank Atlas 1989*).

United States	$19,780
Japan	21,040
West Germany	18,530
Argentina	2,640
Brazil	2,280
Mexico	1,820
Chile	1,510
Peru (1987)	1,440
Colombia	1,240
Dominican Republic	680
Haiti	360

3. In 1986, the population of developing countries (excluding the Soviet Union, Albania, Bulgaria, Czechoslovakia, the German

Democratic Republic, and Vietnam) was 3.7 billion, of which Latin America and the Caribbean represented 413 million. In 1989, Latin American and Caribbean debt totaled $434 billion vis-à-vis total external debt of developing countries of $1.165 trillion (*Handbook of International Trade and Development Statistics, 1988* [population]; *World Debt Tables, 1989–90* [debt]).

4. During 1987 and 1988, the average inflation rate (GDP deflator) in developing countries in the Western Hemisphere was at least five times the average for developing countries in Asia and Africa (*International Financial Statistics*, yearbook, 1990).

	1987	1988
Asia	8.1%	7.0%
Africa	23.5%	19.0%
Western Hemisphere	108.0%	269.1%

5. For purposes of this discussion, Central America includes Mexico, Guatemala, El Salvador, Honduras, Nicaragua, Costa Rica, and Panama.

6. During the 1980s, the Canadian population grew by 2.5 million to 26.5 million (10 percent) (*Statistical Abstract of the United States, 1989*).

7. In 1980, the combined population of these four countries was 45.6 million, 20 percent of that of the United States. During the 1980s, the 16 percent increase added 7.4 million (32.7 percent of the U.S. addition of 22.6 million) (*Statistical Abstract of the United States, 1989*).

8. Included here are Cuba, Haiti, Puerto Rico, Jamaica, and Trinidad and Tobago. Over the 10 years ended 1990, their combined population increased from 21.6 million to 24.3 million (12.5 percent) (*Statistical Abstract of the United States, 1989*).

9. In 1980, the combined populations of Mexico, Guatemala, El Salvador, Honduras, Nicaragua, Costa Rica, Panama, Columbia, Venezuela, Ecuador, Peru, and Brazil were 282.9 million. The average rate of growth during the 1980s was 24.76 percent. Accordingly, the expected and actual 1990 populations are (in millions) (*Statistical Abstract of the United States, 1989*):

Expected population (282.9 x 1.2476)	352.9
Actual population	359.6
Difference	6.7

10. From 1961 through 1987, the following regions accounted for most of the 11.9 million immigrants to the United States (in millions)

(*Statistical Abstract of the United States, 1989*):

Latin America and the Caribbean	4.6
Asia	4.0
Europe	2.5

11.   In 1986, residents of these cities totaled 6.8 million (*Statistical Abstract of the United States, 1989*):

Los Angeles	3,259 thousand
Miami	374 thousand
Fort Lauderdale	149 thousand
Chicago	3,010 thousand

12.   Gross domestic investment includes funds spent to add to a country's fixed productive assets and increases in inventories.

13.   Net commercial loans and international bond issues (new financing less reductions in debt outstanding) in 1985 through 1989 reflect much more attention to Europe and to Asia than in the early 1980s ("International Bond Issues," April 1990).

	Net flows (billions)	
	1983–1984	*1985–1989*
Africa	5.7	−1.5
Latin America	18.9	−7.3
Europe	−0.3	7.2
Asia	22.0	49.4

14.   Gross national product is the value of all goods and services produced within a country plus income from abroad less payments made to nonresidents.

15.   This total includes net government and nongovernmental loans (from all sources), direct investment, portfolio investment (stock and bonds), and short-term capital. Note that the discussion of external financing above referred only to commercial loans and international bond issues.

16.   In 1980 outstanding external debt stood at $242.7 billion. By 1989, the total had risen to $434.1 (*World Debt Tables, 1989–90*).

17.   At the end of 1988, the sum of equity capital and loan loss reserve for the 63 banks in New York, California, and Illinois with assets in excess of $1 billion was $49.5 billion, $18.3 billion, and $6.9 billion, respectively (Federal Deposit Insurance Corporation, *Statistics on Banking*, 1988).

18.   Total assets of the large banks in these states was $975.9 billion at the end of 1988 (Federal Deposit Insurance Corporation,

Statistics on Banking, 1988).

19.   At 5 percent annually, $239 billion grows to $634 billion [$239(1.05)^{20} = $634].

20.   After 20 years, the components and the ratio would have changed in the following manner:

Debt:	($634 bil.) (1.11)^{20} = $5,111.5 bil.
GNP:	($852 bil.) (1.164)^{20} = $17,762.3 bil.
Debt to GNP:	$5,111.5 / $17,762.3 = 0.2878

2

The Politics of
Economics in Japan

JAPANESE DOMINANCE IN WORLD
TRADE AND FINANCE

In 1989, Japan exported merchandise worth $270 billion, resulting in a merchandise trade surplus of $77 billion. These shipments brought total Japanese exports for the seven years ended 1989 to $1.45 trillion and corresponding surpluses to $493 billion. The magnitude of this economic activity is not easy to comprehend. However, its meaning becomes somewhat clearer when one considers how small Japan is geographically. If the value of exports was evenly spread over Japanese soil, these figures indicate that every square mile produced an average of over $10 million in exports during the seven-year period. Further, these exports represent 17 percent or less of the country's total economic activity.

To put this in perspective, while U.S. exports over the same period totaled $1.79 trillion, corresponding merchandise trade balances amounted to deficits of $847 billion. Geographically, U.S. export activity yielded an average of only $540,000 per square mile during the seven years ended 1989. In other words, per square mile export productivity in Japan is 20 times that of the United States. Of course, one possible explanation might be that exports play a smaller role in the U.S. economy, that is, exports range from 7 percent to 9 percent of total U.S. economic activity, versus 17 percent or so in Japan. However, in order for the United States to be as productive as Japan, American exports would have to represent less than 1 percent of the total output of goods and services.[1]

This dominance in international trade activity translates directly into phenomenal growth in Japan's share of the world's wealth. The central bank and other financial institutions in Japan now oversee more international money than their counterparts in virtually every other country in the world. As shown in Table 2.1, the international reserves of the Bank of Japan amounted to 24.3 billion Special Drawing Rights (SDRs) in 1983 or 10.4 percent of the reserves of all industrialized countries.[2] The central banks of West Germany and the United States commanded substantially more at 44.1 billion and 30.8 billion SDRs, respectively. Nevertheless, by the end of 1989, Japan's international reserves had almost tripled to 64.7 billion SDRs, or a nearly 16 percent share. In contrast, the U.S. share had increased only marginally, and West Germany's proportion declined substantially. Clearly, the balance of power among the industrialized central banks has shifted.

Table 2.2 illustrates a comparable shift in the balance of international power among other financial institutions. At the end of 1983, Japanese banks and other institutions held $109.1 billion in foreign assets. This represented only 6.1 percent of the total held by all industrialized countries. The West German share was lower at 4.2 percent. The major players at that time were the United Kingdom and the United States. London was the birthplace of the Euromarkets that developed rapidly during the 1970s. Further, London was a major international financial center long before World War I. The 27.2 percent

TABLE 2.1
International Reserves of the Central Banks of Japan, the United States, and West Germany, 1983 and 1989

	1983		1989	
	Amount (1)	% (2)	Amount (1)	% (2)
Japan	SDR 24.6	10.4%	SDR 64.7	15.8%
United States	30.8	13.1	57.5	14.0
West Germany	44.1	18.8	49.5	12.1
All industrialized nations	SDR 234.6	100.0%	SDR 410.0	100.0%

Notes: (1) in billions of Special Drawing Rights (SDRs). At the end of 1983 and 1989, unit SDR value was $1.04695 and $1.31416, respectively; (2) percentage of international reserves held by industrialized countries.

Source: Amounts: International Monetary Fund. *International Financial Statistics*, May 1990, p. 49. Percentages: Author's calculations.

TABLE 2.2

Foreign Assets of Commercial Banks and Other Financial Institutions in Selected Industrialized Countries, 1983 and 1989

	1983		1989	
	Amount (1)	% (2)	Amount (1)	% (2)
Japan	$ 109.1	6.1%	$ 842.1	19.6%
United States	433.1	24.3	656.4	15.3
West Germany	74.8	4.2	295.3	6.9
United Kingdom	485.2	27.2	924.0	21.5
All industrialized nations	$1,784.0	100.0%	$4,299.6	100.0%

Notes: (1) in billions of U.S. dollars; (2) percentage of foreign assets held by the financial institutions (excluding monetary authorities) of all industrialized nations.

Sources: Amounts: International Monetary Fund. *International Financial Statistics,* May 1990, p. 53. Percentages: Author's calculations.

share of the United Kingdom in international finance is, thus, not surprising. Likewise, New York banks engineered and pioneered most of the financial instruments that are now the mainstays of international finance. The 24.3 percent of the United States is consistent with this tradition.

However, by the end of 1989, the United Kingdom represented 21.5 percent of the foreign assets of financial institutions in industrialized countries, down from over 27 percent. The change in the United States was even more dramatic, with a decline from 24.3 percent to 15.3 percent. While West Germany inched forward slightly, the largest gains were realized by Japan. Its slightly more than 6-percent share of foreign assets more than tripled to just under 20 percent. In only six years, Japan surpassed the United States in international banking circles and now seriously rivals London, the home of the Euromarket.

None of these observations suggests that world economic activity and finance are developing in a uniform, global fashion. Japan is clearly outperforming the United States. How could Japan outpace the United States in this way in less than 50 years after its World War II defeat? It is perhaps because the United States has seen what it wanted to see after 1945.

Postwar occupation forces attempted to structure the new Japan like a mini-America with an antitrust legal structure, a less-concentrated business configuration, a Glass-Steagall-style banking system, and a cooperative international posture. However, as shown in the following section, none of these characteristics describe Japan today. At the same time, it cannot be denied that Japan is a powerful world economic force. The question that arises is whether Japan can be expected to be a socially responsible global economic partner with the rest of the industrialized nations. The concept of globalism is defined as a "policy or outlook that is worldwide in scope."[3] In the context of business, such a worldwide outlook should apply to trade and investment policies and practices in order for them to be considered global. Using this simple rule of thumb, Japanese economic behavior fails on every front to qualify as "global."

UNDERSTANDING JAPAN

The events of the past two decades have taken the United States by surprise because Americans have essentially come to believe their own propaganda of democracy and "fair play," concepts that they hold in high esteem. Because the United States has enjoyed virtually uninterrupted economic expansion since World War II, there seemed to be little need to pay close attention to the manner in which postwar Japan was restructuring itself, particularly since so much of the legal and business framework had been modeled after U.S. systems.

Actually, Japanese development has not mirrored that of the United States. If democracy means that no one sector — government, business, or individuals — receives significantly more preferential treatment than the other, Japan is not democratic. If playing fair means that all parties in the game operate under the same rules, Japan also is not fair. The country is strongly nationalistic with unmistakable tendencies toward imperialism. The Japanese perception of the world is not of a more or less global economy, but rather of decidedly regionalized economics with Japan at the center of the most important region.

More specifically, history, both distant and more recent, suggests at least five conclusions about the Japanese view of the world.

1. The function of the rest of the world is to serve the needs of the Japanese.
2. Even within his own society, the average Japanese person is a kind of natural resource for more powerful sectors.
3. What the Japanese say and what they do is not consistently the same.

4. The Japanese concept of world economics and trade is highly regionalized.

5. The Japanese "empire" already has begun to spread to other Asian countries.

JAPANESE DEVELOPMENT BEFORE WORLD WAR II

As early as the fifth century, the Japanese borrowed from other societies. At that time, visitors to China brought back the ideograms first used to document Shinto (religious) beliefs and customs. Central to Shinto religion, indigenous to Japan, is that the sun-goddess, the most exalted deity, is the ancestor of the country's line of emperors. Thus, early Shinto beliefs were conducive to the development of a privileged class. By the eighth century, a centralized state under imperial rule was well on its way to formation.

However, imperial rule was interrupted by a period of feudalism that was enforced by military rule. It was at this time that the much-heralded samurai warriors emerged. During its feudal period, Japan remained essentially isolated from the rest of the world. However, in 1854 when U.S. Naval Officer Matthew Perry persuaded the ruling family to allow Americans access to Japanese ports, the country's outward focus began in earnest. The Meiji Restoration of 1868 placed formal power with Emperor Meiji and the economic development of Japan commenced as the samurai maintained civil order.

The Japanese traveled to England to study the British navy and merchant marine. The army and medical practice of Germany also were objects of their curiosity. In France, law and government were of particular interest. The United States offered an opportunity to learn about business.

The lessons of Europe and the U.S. were well learned. A parliamentary form of government (the Diet), along with a constitutional monarchy, was established and Western industrialism took hold. However, unlike the United States and Britain, for example, Japan possessed few natural resources. Accordingly, the ruling class used the then centuries-old samurai tradition to help procure what was needed. In 1894 Japan invaded China, retaining what is now Taiwan at the conclusion of that two-year war. Taiwan represented a reliable source of foodstuffs as the Japanese people turned to more industrial pursuits. Mineral-rich Korea also had been invaded during the conflict.

Japan and Russia locked horns over both Korea and timber- and mineral-rich Manchuria in 1904. Japan formally annexed Korea in 1910 and established a puppet government in Manchuria in 1932, after feigning provocation by the Chinese. A full war between the two countries erupted in 1937. Cities near the coast, Tianjin, Peking (now Beijing), Shanghai, and Nanjing fell. These cities were strategically important because they provided a channel for the raw materials and other goods that Japan wanted. Of course, the 1941 invasion of Pearl Harbor merged the Sino-Japanese conflict with World War II and ultimately led to the end of Japan's military aggression.

Meanwhile, at home, the structure of business enterprise followed strong family lines — corporate imperialism. "Zaibatsus" were, perhaps, the world's first multinational conglomerates. These family-owned, bank-centered holding companies dominated Japanese business during the first 40 years of this century. From suppliers to manufacturers to distributors, the zaibatsus controlled all vertical activity in a wide range of industries. Almost all corporate common stock and bonds were held by zaibatsu family members.

Coordination and financing were the responsibilities of the zaibatsu's bank. Banks proved to be an effective conduit for industrial funding during this period, drawing funds even from captured territories. For example, the first modern commercial bank in Korea was Japanese. In 1876, Daiichi Ginko began operations in Korea. At the conclusion of the Russo-Japanese War in 1905, Daiichi Ginko bank notes became Korea's legal tender even before formal annexation in 1910. Thus, occupied territory became the source of not only natural resources but also financial resources in the form of savings deposited in the banking system.

After its creation in 1882, the Bank of Japan (central bank) kept a watchful eye over the operations of the Western-style banks, particularly the larger ones. Although there were over 2,000 banks at the turn of the century, the Bank of Japan acted as lender of last resort to only 40 or 50 and these were concentrated in Tokyo, Osaka, Kyoto, and Yokohama. When assistance was needed, the Bank of Japan made loans to these larger banks at below-market rates accepting extremely illiquid zaibatsu stocks or bonds as collateral. Thus, even the ostensibly Western-style banking structure was characterized by imperialist tendencies and a class system.

The coalitions formed between business, banking, government, and the military were strong and deeply rooted. The spiritual element of Shinto, the state religion until 1945, lent credibility to the elitism of pre-World War II Japan. In this context, the assertion that Japan was democratic or played fair appears questionable at best.

It is interesting to note that these natural resource and banking themes have developed in Japan's investment patterns in the United

States. Of the $70 billion total (as of 1989), Japanese held investments of $10 billion in U.S. banks and other financial institutions, that is, 14 percent of the total. In contrast, the European Communities (EC) had a total 1989 direct investment position in the United States of $235 billion, with only 6 percent in financial institutions. The combination of primary and fabricated metal manufacturing, machinery manufacturing and wholesale trade represented 41 percent of Japan's direct investment in the United States, but only 19 percent of EC investment.

In a manner not completely unlike the colonial Korean experience, Japanese manufacturing operations in the United States channel output through Japanese wholesale trading companies with transactions financed by Japanese banks. The territorial nature of their culture is also reflected in their investment patterns in the United States. While Japanese direct investment in all areas represents 17 percent of total foreign direct investment, Japanese real estate holdings are 40 percent of all foreign-owned land.

Diplomatically, the United States may consider itself important in Japan's economic structure. However, in terms of capital investment, the primary functions that the United States appears best suited for are basic manufacturing and expanding the sphere of Japanese farm and other land ownership.

THE NEW JAPANESE CORPORATE STRUCTURE

In 1952, after seven years of occupation, social restructuring, and substantial amounts of financial aid, the United States began to view Japan as a democratic and pacifist nation. The previous century of Japanese history seemed not to matter anymore. Perhaps, the guilt of nuclear attack prevented a more objective assessment. After all, laying waste to Hiroshima and Nagasaki and maintaining a healthy skepticism about the Japanese people may not have seemed fair. Forgive and forget may have been more palatable for American tastes.

Whatever the reasons, the United States failed to recognize the old trends in the new Japan. As part of the Allied restructuring, zaibatsus were dismantled. Fifty family members relinquished most of the stock of 83 holding companies with 4,500 subsidiaries. Over 200 million shares of stock with a value of ¥9.1 billion changed hands. In addition, corporate ranks were reorganized with each official permitted to serve no more than one corporation.

Once the occupation ended in 1952, however, old alliances were reinstituted via a new form of association that satisfied the letter of the law, if not the spirit. Under the zaibatsu arrangement, one holding company had owned all the shares of each subsidiary company. Under the new "keiretsu" arrangement, each company in the group owns a small percentage (originally 1 percent to 3 percent) of the shares of every other group member. The net effect is identical in both cases, that is, a closely knit corporate group with virtually no outside influence. This is a good example of the Japanese propensity to appear to be conciliatory with respect to a disputed issue while simultaneously achieving a self-serving end result. The central board of directors no longer exists, but the presidents of each of the major member firms meet with regularity on an informal basis to consider strategic and other issues. Substantively, there is little difference between zaibatsus and keiretsus.

If U.S. observers had watched these developments more closely, it would have been clear to them that the Japanese are not averse to saying one thing and doing another. There have been any number of commitments by Japan to improve the trade balance between the two countries, for example. These commitments have been essentially unfulfilled. The 1983 imbalance of $18.5 billion grew to $52.5 billion in 1987, only to decline slightly to $49.4 billion in 1989. While Japanese exports to the United States continued to balloon, Japanese imports from the United States increased from $24.7 billion in 1983 to only $31.7 billion in 1987, an increase of $7 billion (28 percent) over a four-year period.

Over the same period, however, Japanese imports from the EC grew by $10 billion from a considerably smaller base of $7.6 billion. Thus, Japanese trade officials would have the United States understand that the Japanese economy could absorb only a 28 percent increase in imports from the United States, while a 132 percent increase in EC imports was completely manageable. Since the United States and the EC are comparable in terms of degree of industrialization and product mix, this disparity is not easily reconciled with the concept of globalization.

BANKS RESUME THEIR POSITION OF POWER

Business cartels are not the only examples of Japanese lip service to the democratic process. Government policy after the war has continued to favor business interests over those of individuals and the banking system has been instrumental in this economic engineering.

Initially the center of the new keiretsu was the trading company. These members were, perhaps, natural choices because the most pressing need was perceived to be dependable resource availability and adequate distribution channels for finished goods. However, as these challenges were met, financing corporate ventures moved to the top of the list of priorities. Predictably, the keiretsu banks reclaimed their position of dominance.

The Japanese government encouraged the preeminence of banks by structuring the country's financial system to assure the achievement of national goals. The savings process was encouraged, and rightly so. In industrialized economics, it is not uncommon for household or individual savings to be mobilized for investment in those areas most needed.

Using the United States as but one example, early commercial bank deposits were reinvested in working capital loans to industry. The thrift industry emerged to provide sources of housing finance and consumer loans. The insurance industry mobilized savings to provide individuals with adequate protection of life and livelihood while offering long-term financing to industry in the interim. The stock and bond markets made it possible for both institutions and individuals to share in the fortunes (and sometimes misfortunes) of industry.

These U.S. market mechanisms grew out of societal need and the forces of supply and demand. Along the way, the government provided special inducements for high-priority activities. Tax-deductibility of mortgage interest encouraged housing finance. Preferential capital gains tax rates were intended to promote investment in capital assets. These and other incentives were intended to facilitate activities, not to control them.

However, the Japanese government, rather than Japanese society, decided how savings would be gathered and reinvested. The first step was to establish compelling motivations to save. This was accomplished by making the savings process tax-free. Interest on bank deposits, government securities, and postal savings accounts was tax-exempt.[4] Such tax-exemption helps to explain the high savings rate in Japan, where roughly 20 percent of disposable income is saved.

In and of themselves, these savings motivations are positive government measures to spur economic investment by those institutions with whom individuals entrusted their savings. However, other government measures served to discourage alternative forms of savings. For example, historically, common stock dividends have not been subject simply to taxation, but also to withholding tax. In other words, the government has taken its share right off the top. The result has been that the effective yield from common stock is lower than the bank deposit yield. Clearly, this is a disincentive for stock ownership.

Further, corporations were expected to issue new stock at artificially low par values rather than market values. Worse yet, issuing firms were expected to pay annual dividends of 10 percent to 15 percent of par. Since interest payments on debt were tax-deductible for firms but dividend payments were not, corporate debt represented much lower cost financing.[5]

The combination of savings incentives aimed toward debt financing, disincentives for stock issuance, and direct government controls of corporate finance ensured that the one-way flow of Japanese funds was from individuals through banks and the postal savings system to those industries that the government designated. Housing finance did not develop. No meaningful consumer finance materialized. Few infrastructure projects for the individual were initiated, only those for industry. Industry and government worked together to control the Japanese economy.

The most important power brokers, of course, were the banks. Because of the grossly underdeveloped nature of money and capital markets, industry depended on banks for financing. Banks, in turn, depended on the Bank of Japan to fund the always-excessive demand for industrial loans. The Bank of Japan faithfully responded with cheap money, on the condition that recipient banks, in turn, made low-interest loans to those industries that government designated.

Immediately after the war, core industries received the most attention — coal, electric power, fertilizers, chemicals, steel, and shipbuilding. As these industries matured, the focus turned to import substitution in areas such as electronics and automobiles. "Growth" was the byword and banks financed that growth under the careful supervision of Japanese government.

Exports became the key to growth. During the 1950s and 1960s, the government promoted exporting firms in several ways. Tax-free reserves could be set aside if a firm attempted to develop an export market. In a rare case of support for small business, government established the Japan External Trade Organization to provide foreign market research for small firms. In addition, the Export-Import Bank was organized.

While the government consciously structured Japan's financial system to achieve its agenda, the banks did not hesitate to exert pressure to perpetuate and build their own empires. As major shareholders in the industrial firms of their keiretsus and holders of the purse strings, banks effectively discouraged alternative forms of domestic corporate finance such as stocks and bonds. Even the government, with its clearly stated policy of export promotion, prevented all but the largest Japanese firms from obtaining more competitively priced funds overseas for many years. It was not until 1977 that the Ministry of Finance liberalized the issue of Eurobonds by all firms. The Ministry now has also allowed other elements of the financial markets to develop.

However, it cannot be denied that collaboration between the government and the banking system made Japanese industry more heavily dependent on banks than any other industrialized country. As a direct result, Japanese institutions now dominate the ranks of the world's largest banking organizations.

This concentration of banking power is having a profound effect on the flow of bank funds. When U.S. banks were still dominant, the balance of loans to developing countries was much less lopsided than in later years. Even after the Mexican debt scare in 1982, $21 billion in bank financing went to developing countries in the Western Hemisphere during the two-year period ended 1984. A roughly equivalent $17 billion was awarded to Asian developing countries. However, from 1985 through 1988, as Japanese banks rose to the top of world finance, loans to developing countries in the Western Hemisphere declined by $8 billion, while loans to developing countries in Asia increased by $23 billion. Is it a coincidence that the shift of power to Japanese banks occurred at the same time that bank financing to the developing countries of the Western Hemisphere dried up?

NO APOLOGIES

The internal economic engineering of Japan should suggest something about the way that Japan views the rest of the world. The business and government sectors are not likely to regard Americans or Germans or Soviets with any higher esteem than they do Japanese consumers and workers. Conventional wisdom notwithstanding, the postwar business sector has exploited average Japanese workers almost to the extent that its prewar counterpart exploited Koreans. Twelve-hour workdays and six-day workweeks are the norm. Even so, neither government nor industry has seriously addressed the issue of adequate, affordable housing. Competitively priced food is also not a high priority, despite the fact that domestic agricultural industry represents no more than 2 percent to 3 percent of total Japanese economic activity.

Perhaps the most revealing form of negligence with respect to Japanese workers is the underdeveloped pension system. The celebrated lifetime job in Japan is more often than not terminated with little or no financial provision for retirement. Female employees, even though they may work full time, are considered temporary employees and not eligible for pension benefits. Lump-sum payments upon retirement are the most common form of Japanese retirement benefits. In contrast, the most common pension plan in the United States guarantees a minimum level of retirement income.

In 1986, private pension plans in the United States held $1.4 trillion dollars in assets. In the same year, Japanese private pensions funds held only $121 billion. As Japan has moved forward to dominate industrial and banking circles, there has been much less commitment to economically empower the average worker.

As lopsided as this might seem in the United States, it is a non-issue in Japan. The course of action that will accomplish the goals of the power elite is the course of action that is adopted. Nor is this attitude new, cultivated in the last five years or so. This is an attitude that has been manifested since the Meiji Restoration. Even the devastation of World War II did little to disrupt this train of thought. In the 1950s, the United States encouraged a policy of containment with respect to the new Communist regime in China. Japan's official posture was consistent with this policy. However, the Japanese foreign affairs ministry devised a plan referred to as "seikaibunri," that is, the separation of politics from economic activity.

Simply stated, Japan pursued trade with China while maintaining that the two countries had no official contact. In a general context, this is, at best, a semantic difference. In the context of Japanese culture, it is an outrageous assertion. In a country where government policy is almost 100 percent industrial policy to the exclusion of households and consumers, to suggest that trade was not an official activity constitutes a blatant disregard for the truth, even by Japanese standards. Nevertheless, seikaibunri accomplished the desired outcome.

The Japanese have even begun to subtly rewrite history. The Ministry of Education has changed the description of Japanese involvement in World War II. Textbook passages that once stated that Japan "invaded" China and other parts of Asia now state that Japan "entered" these regions. Although the change sparked protest throughout Asia, it better served the self-image of the Japanese elite.

JAPAN: OUR PARTNER IN GLOBALIZATION?

In its naiveté, the United States continues to negotiate with Japan on trade and other issues under the assumption that democracy and fair play are the ground rules. From the Japanese perspective, the true ground rules reduce to one simple axiom: Japan should work to enrich Japanese industry and finance.

Several implications are suggested by the past and present economic behavior of Japan.

1. Japanese investment is now and will continue to be concentrated primarily within Asia.
2. The new frontier for Asian exports is Europe.
3. Whatever meaningful liberalization of Japanese imports occurs will be reserved to accommodate other Asian countries and the EC.
4. Japan will continue to avoid investing or trading in South American markets until the United States somehow resolves the Latin American debt problems.

Clearly, none of these likely developments bodes well for the United States or globalization.

Investing Close to Home

As early as 1965, government policy emphasized not only exports but also direct foreign investment, especially to acquire raw materials sources. There is now a strong functional relationship between Japan and other Asian countries. These relationships are apparent when trends in investment flow, Japanese aid to developing countries, and trade flows are examined. Each of these provides evidence of the economic commitment within the area. From January 1984 through June 1987, Japan made direct foreign investments of $6.6 billion in Hong Kong, Korea, Taiwan, Singapore, Indonesia, Malaysia, and Thailand. Generally, the later investments exceeded the earlier ones. Further, the pace of investment has quickened even more so recently, totaling over $12 billion in 1989 alone. This is five times the U.S. investment in Asia during 1989.

These investments mean that keiretsus are now spreading throughout Asia. Japan is purchasing the resources and manpower that it once obtained via military aggression.

Official development assistance (ODA) is the government's form of investment. Of course, ODA theoretically is intended to assist countries in the development process with, presumably, no strings attached. However, it is noteworthy that historically, 70 percent of Japanese ODA has been paid to Asian countries, and 10 percent to the Middle East, South America, and Africa each. Since Japan is now the world's largest ODA donor, the 70 percent Asian share is not an insignificant amount.

The flow of trade is, perhaps, the most revealing evidence of Japanese intentions. Japan is a major supplier of manufactured goods used in industry for developing Asian countries. Large shares of its total output flow to these countries. In 1987, such goods (and the percentage that exports to developing Asian countries represented of total Japanese exports) included noncotton textiles (38 percent), iron and steel plate and sheet metal (52 percent), iron and steel tubes and pipes (31 percent), nonelectric power tools (25 percent), and electric power machines (38 percent). In the categories of chemicals and basic manufactuers Japan ran a $10.2 billion trade surplus with these countries.

The materials are being used by both Japanese foreign subsidiaries and indigenous firms in other Asian countries to create huge merchandise trade surplus with the United States. To a lesser extent, China is also being brought into the flow. Raw and intermediate materials from Japan and China are processed into export goods targeted for the United States and EC.

In 1983, Hong Kong, Singapore, and Korea had a net trade deficit of $14.4 billion with Japan and China. In the same year, their U.S./EC trade balance was a surplus of $6.8 billion. By 1987, the Japan/China deficit had grown to $20.4 billion and the U.S./EC surplus to $25.2 billion.

Thailand, Indonesia, and Malaysia exhibit a similar pattern, albeit to a lesser extent. Their China/Japan trade balance was a surplus of $3 billion in 1983, but declined to $2.2 billion in 1987. However, the U.S./EC surplus of $91 million increased to $3.5 billion in 1987. While the numbers are smaller, these countries have a lower wage structure and probably will enjoy significant transfers of manufacturing activity in the future.

Other developing regions do not receive the benefit of this interaction with Japan. Total 1987 trade (imports and exports) between Japan and other Asian/Pacific nations amounted to $137 billion. This was actually higher than Japan's total trade with North America ($134 billion). However, in the same year, trade flows between Japan and Africa were $9 billion, between Japan and South America $7 billion. With abundant natural resources in both Africa and South America, it is difficult to justify these large differences.

It is apparent that Japan has very strong regional preferences. Nevertheless, one nagging resource problem continues to persist. Energy is a seemingly never-ending resource problem for Japan. Given this fact, it is even more difficult to understand why Japan was so reluctant to assist the United States in the Persian Gulf conflict in which Iraqi President Saddam Hussein invaded Kuwait, effectively shutting off Japan's (and others') access to the crude oil in both countries.

Yet here, too, Japan appears to be working to assure its empire of sources closer to home. Japan is now the largest joint venture oil developer in China, surpassing the United States. Ironically, after the June 1989 Tiananmen Square massacre, Japan was the first to speak up and admonish the rest of the world not to isolate China because of what had happened. One suspects that this spirit of forgiveness had more to do with trade alliances than with philosophical concerns.

One also might suspect China will not be the only beneficiary of Japan's oil exploration efforts. Relations between the Soviet Union and Japan have begun to mellow and with this softening of hard lines, there is already a joint venture on Sakhalin peninsula for oil exploration. In characteristic fashion, Japan is likely to fully exploit any opportunity to gain access to Soviet oil that arises.

In its pursuit of energy independence, Japan has elected to cover Indonesia's entire international trade deficit out of the goodness of its collective heart. That Indonesia (and Malaysia, as well) is a major oil producer, of course, is a fact that has not been lost on the generous donor.

Coal is another significant energy need for Japan. Presently, Australia supplies roughly half of Japanese coal consumption. To help bring remaining coal sources closer to home, the Export-Import Bank began to invest in Chinese coal mines in the early 1980s.

These efforts are aimed at energy self-sufficiency. They are joint ventures, that is, ownership projects. It is quite likely that, within the next decade, Japan will own a major oil-producing company in Asia or the Soviet Union and significant coal reserves. Thus, there would be no reason for Japan to be responsive to a call from the United States for assistance in the Persian Gulf.

The New European Frontier

Why should Japan have been so accommodating by increasing its imports from Europe in recent years? Simply stated, there is an expectation that the EC represents the new growth market for Japanese exports. Harmonization of trade laws in 1992, together with German reunification and the conversion to market economics of Eastern European countries, suggest that incremental European demand for Japanese goods may be higher than American demand, at least long-term. In the meantime, it may be good strategy to show good faith by increasing importation of European goods.

However, Japan is not alone in its aspirations to grow within the European market. Germany sees itself as the economic leader of Europe. It is quite likely that Japan will have to fight for every point of European market share. Up to this time, the two countries have had little reason for conflict. Germany exported only 10 percent of its goods to the United States, while the United States represented Japan's largest market. On the other hand, roughly half of Germany's exports stayed within the EC. As recently as 1983, the EC was the destination for only 4 percent ($6 billion) of Japan's exports. However, by 1987 exports to the EC represented a 17 percent share ($38 billion) of Japanese exports. As this proportion continues to increase, trade tensions are also likely to grow.

In addition, this pressure will be exerted by the Asian subsidiaries of Japan, Inc. Exports from six Asian locations (Hong Kong, Korea, Singapore, Indonesia, Malaysia, and Thailand) to the EC totaled $13 billion in 1983. Four years later, the total was $24 billion.

EC imports from these seven countries (including Japan) rose in four years from $31 billion to $62 billion, a 100 percent increase. This compares favorably with the $62 billion (90 percent) increase in exports to the United States over the same period. Such EC increases were sustained before the fall of communism and German reunification. Under these circumstances, there is little wonder that Japan has opened its domestic markets to a greater flow of EC goods.

Reserving Space for Asia

At the same time, Japan probably realizes that some time will elapse before the European markets have matured sufficiently to absorb the full export potential of its Asian "subsidiaries." Thus, while the country ostensibly encourages its citizens to purchase more consumer goods — that is, imports — U.S. companies continue to experience difficulty placing goods on the Japanese market. As history has illustrated, very little happens by coincidence in Japan. These difficulties continue to occur because the United States is viewed as a trading partner of declining, not increasing, importance.

Avoiding Latin America

In fact, Japan probably sees the entire Western Hemisphere as a declining market. This is particularly true of South America. The minimal levels of trade with this region may be attributable to both its distance from Asia and its financial distress.

In the 1970s, OPEC trade surpluses were recycled to developing nations through commercial banks, with U.S. banks leading the way. Subsequently, high interest rates and slumping world commodity prices have caused repayment to be exceedingly difficult, if not impossible, in many cases. Nevertheless, the natural resources, particularly in South America, still remain.

Now it is Japan that is accumulating the trade surpluses. However, Japan is ignoring virtually all developing countries outside Asia. No offers to cover trade deficits are forthcoming (as is the case in Indonesia). With respect to Latin America, Japan no doubt realizes that the United States will be forced to resolve the region's debt crisis. To do otherwise would ensure that the United States will have an insurmountable immigration problem, as desperate citizens in the South seek a better chance of survival in the North.

With the distance that separates Japan from Latin America, the former is probably content to let this process run its course. Once the debt crisis is resolved, Japan will step forward in characteristic fashion to develop yet another export market.

Strong Regionalization Implied

There appears to be little doubt that Japan is not interested in becoming a full-fledged global market participant. There may not be much that the United States can do to change the Japanese perception of the world, but with a somewhat more careful analysis of the situation, perhaps the United States can change its perception of Japan. What is true in the military sense is no less true in the economic sense. One should always attempt to know thy enemy.

NOTES

1. In Japan, if exports represent 17 percent of GNP and each square mile produced $10 million in exports, then, during this period, total productivity averaged $58.8 million per square mile ($10 million ÷ 0.17). If the same average total output applied to the United States, the observed average exports of $540,000 would be only 0.9 percent of the total ($0.540 million ÷ $58.8 million).

2. International reserves are composed of foreign currency, monetary gold, and IMF fund balances and special drawing rights (SDRs).

3.   David B. Guralnik, ed., *Webster's New World Dictionary of the American Language,* 2d college edition (William Collins and World Publishing, 1978).

4.   Each of these investments is subject to limitation with respect to amount invested in order to qualify for tax-exempt treatment. However, if a Japanese citizen were to acquire the maximum tax-free amount in each available instrument, the total qualifying investment would be ¥14 million.

5.   The U.S. treatment of interest payments and dividends is the same as Japan's. However, the other conditions for stock issue do not apply.

3

The Dynamics of
Asia Outside Japan

JAPAN AS THE ECONOMIC LOCOMOTIVE OF ASIA

There appears to be little disagreement that Japan is currently the major investor in other Asian countries when official development assistance ((DA), foreign direct investment (FDI), and loans are all considered. What is less well understood, perhaps, is the extent to which Japan has fulfilled this role for more than 20 years.[1] In other words, the dramatic changes in Asian prosperity in the 1980s have been largely fueled by Japanese assistance and investment, with few significant economic or political alliances being stimulated outside of the region.

As shown in Table 3.1, at the beginning of the 1970s, annual ODA from developed countries in the Pacific region to eight developing nations within the region totaled $797 million. Of this total, the United States and Japan were the largest contributors at $447 million and $308 million, respectively, with the remaining $42 million coming from Australia ($29 million), Canada ($11 million), and New Zealand ($2 million). In other words, a total of 95 percent came from the United States (56 percent) and Japan (39 percent). The major beneficiaries were Indonesia, South Korea, and, to a lesser extent, the Philippines.

Ten years later, in the early 1980s, total ODA to the eight developing countries had increased to $1.14 billion annually. Contributions from Australia ($80 million), Canada ($31 million), and New Zealand ($8 million) had all been stepped up such that an additional $77 million was paid. In contrast, the U.S. contribution

TABLE 3.1
Average Annual Official Development Assistance within the Pacific Region, 1970–1972 and 1980–1982 (in millions of dollars)

		Donors		
Recipients	Japan	U.S.	Canada Australia & New Zealand	Total
1970–1972				
Taiwan	$ 4.4	$ (2.7)	$ ---	$ 1.7
South Korea	107.9	193.3	1.4	302.6
Singapore	6.3	---	1.3	7.6
Hong Kong	0.1	---	---	0.1
Malaysia	9.2	3.0	6.9	19.1
Indonesia	113.6	190.3	26.6	330.5
Thailand	16.0	31.0	5.2	52.2
The Philippines	50.8	32.0	0.8	83.6
	$308.3	$446.9	$42.2	$797.4
1980–1982				
Taiwan	$ (1.1)	$ (8.0)	$ ---	$ (9.1)
South Korea	125.2	7.0	0.5	132.7
Singapore	7.3	---	2.1	9.4
Hong Kong	1.5	---	0.1	1.6
Malaysia	68.5	1.0	9.5	79.0
Indonesia	314.8	97.3	71.3	483.4
Thailand	191.5	19.0	19.3	229.8
The Philippines	147.0	53.0	16.4	216.4
	$854.7	$169.3	$119.2	$1,143.2

Sources: Japan, U.S., Total: Tan, Augustine H. H. and Basant Kapur, Editors. *Pacific Growth and Financial Interdependence*. North Sydney, Australia: Allen & Unwin, 1986. p. 76. Canada, Australia, and New Zealand, author's calculations based on: Tan, Augustine H. H. and Basant Kapur, Editors. *Pacific Growth and Financial Interdependence*. North Sydney, Australia: Allen & Unwin, 1986, p. 76.

declined from $447 million to $169 million, or 62 percent. The largest drop in U.S. aid was to South Korea, the second largest to Indonesia.

By far, the most significant source of increases in official aid was Japan. By the early 1980s, total Japanese contributions to these eight countries stood at $885 million, 75 percent of the total and almost three times the amount ten years earlier. The greatest beneficiaries of increased aid were Indonesia, Thailand, the Philippines, and Malaysia. It is no coincidence that these countries offer a low wage structure ideally suited for manufacturing operations.[2] Of course, Indonesia and Malaysia have the added attraction of significant energy reserves. Japanese foreign policy, like every other form of public policy, is aimed at furthering the goals of Japanese industry. And Japanese industry has found these regions to be most enticing means of expansion.

Also, in the early 1980s, Japanese firms held commanding shares of foreign direct investment. Table 3.2 contains a breakdown of FDI in the region at this time. The U.S. share was significantly greater than Japan's in the Philippines (where a large U.S. military presence is maintained), Hong Kong, and Singapore. The latter two locations have been particularly aggressive in modeling their economic systems in such a way that their functions as entrepôts (warehousing and distribution centers) have placed them squarely in the center of international flows of goods, services, and capital. The large U.S. share of FDI is, at least partially, attributable to the ease with which foreign investments can be initiated in Singapore and Hong Kong. In addition, cultural and language barriers have been less difficult to overcome.

However, in South Korea, Malaysia, Indonesia, and Thailand, Japanese firms owned more productive facilities than any other single country in the late 1970s and early 1980s. Further, even at this time, these countries' foreign investment patterns showed other signs of strong regional integration. When the shares of FDI of other Asian firms are added to those of Japan, total Asian investment in Malaysia (61 percent), South Korea (52 percent), Thailand (49 percent), and Indonesia (47 percent) represented on the order of one-half of all FDI.

Of course, the fact still remains that Japan generally has been the chief supplier of direct investment capital in Asia. The pace of this investment began to accelerate particularly in the early 1970s. As can be seen in Table 3.3, Japanese FDI in Asia amounted to $751 million during the 20 years ended 1970. Other than the country's investment in North America ($912 million), no other region was the recipient of more Japanese investment capital.

TABLE 3.2
Foreign Direct Investment in Eight Developing Countries in the Pacific Region in the Early 1980s
(in percent)

| | Investing Countries | | | | | | | | | |
| | Developed Countries | | | | Asian Developing Countries | | | | | |
Recipients	Japan	U.S.	Canada, Australia, New Zealand	Europe	Hong Kong	Singapore	Taiwan	Others	Others Outside Asia	As of
Taiwan	23.6%	29.6%	---%	8.7%	7.7%	---%	---%	---%	30.4%	1983
South Korea	50.6	24.7	---	11.4	1.6	---	---	---	11.7	1981
Singapore	16.4	34.0	---	39.2	---	---	---	---	10.4	1980
Hong Kong	21.7	44.5	3.8	19.6	---	2.7	1.1	3.3	3.3	1980
Malaysia	26.7	11.3	2.6	---	12.7	20.7	0.4	0.2	25.4	1977
Indonesia	34.0	6.7	1.8	16.1	6.9	1.3	0.9	4.0	28.3	1983
Thailand	25.8	10.3	2.8	17.1	5.2	5.3	9.6	2.9	21.0	1984
The Philippines	14.8	53.8	4.2	16.7	5.3	0.6	---	0.3	4.3	1983

Sources: Canada, Australia, New Zealand, and other Asian developing, author's calculations based on: Tan, Augustine H. H. and Basant Kapur, Editors. *Pacific Growth and Financial Interdependence*. North Sydney, Australia: Allen & Unwin, 1986, p. 79 Others: Tan, Augustine H. H. and Basant Kapur, Editors. *Pacific Growth and Financial Interdependence*. North Sydney, Australia: Allen & Unwin, 1986, p. 79.

TABLE 3.3
Foreign Direct Investment by Japan, 1951–1982

(in millions of dollars)

	1951-1970	1971-1976	1977-1982	1951-1982	%(1)
U.S.	$ 701	$ 3,380	$ 9,889	$13,970	26.3%
Canada	211	375	669	1,255	2.4
North America	912	3,755	10,558	15,225	28.7
Taiwan	85	141	253	479	0.9
South Korea	32	657	623	1,312	2.4
Singapore	33	268	1,082	1,383	2.6
Hong Kong	29	418	1,378	1,825	3.4
Malaysia	50	303	411	764	1.4
Indonesia	242	2,467	4,559	7,268	13.7
Thailand	91	137	293	521	1.0
The Philippines	74	281	366	721	1.4
Other	115	40	125	280	0.5
Asia	751	4,712	9,090	14,553	27.3
Latin America	567	2,735	5,550	8,852	16.7
Europe	639	2,215	3,292	6,146	11.6
Australia	210	608	2,064	2,882	5.4
New Zealand	33	76	103	212	0.4
Other	38	128	109	275	0.5
Oceania	281	812	2,276	3,369	6.3
Middle East	334	920	1,225	2,479	4.7
Africa	93	680	1,734	2,507	4.7
	$3,477	$15,829	$33,725	$53,131	100.0%

Note: (1) as a percentage of total Japanese foreign direct investment.
Sources: 1971-1976 and 1977-1982, author's calculations based on: Tan, Augustine H. H. and Basant Kapur, Editors. *Pacific Growth and Financial Interdependence.* North Sydney, Australia: Allen & Unwin, 1986, p. 82. Others: Tan, Augustine H. H. and Basant Kapur, Editors. *Pacific Growth and Financial Interdependence.* North Sydney, Australia: Allen & Unwin, 1986, p. 82.

It should be noted that there is an important distinction between Japanese investment in a developed country and corresponding capital flows to a developing country. The former is more likely to be aimed at gaining technical expertise (in the early postwar years) or at setting up production facilities to evade criticism for excessive trade surpluses (in more recent years). The latter is aimed at satisfying a raw materials resource need. Accordingly, Japanese FDI in a developed country does not create the kind of economic dependence that corresponding investment in a developing country does. While investment in a developed country is intended to exploit its knowledge or to create the illusion of reducing cash flows to Japanese firms, investment in a developing country constitutes partial economic colonization.

The Japanese do not attempt to conceal these motivations. In the 1989 *Japan Economic Almanac,* several references to specific company strategies help to illustrate this point. With respect to obtaining technical expertise, the Japanese government has begun to urge high-tech research and development (R & D) teams to "study foreign ideas and situations to help them come up with greater originality." In the Japanese way of thinking, copying ideas from the competition is completely acceptable — in fact, commendable. In line with this objective, in 1988 Kobe Steel established its first overseas (R & D) institute in London to study polymer-based materials.

In pursuit of frictionless access to the European Communities (EC) markets of 1992, Toyota Motors plans to start producing small-sized cars in Great Britain. The autos will have 80 percent local content. Thus, the British production will be considered locally produced and not violate Japan's agreement to maintain its auto exports to the EC at roughly current levels in terms of EC market share. In any event, the profits will accrue to Japanese shareholders.

NEC Corporation is but one example of the firms that have sought to colonize developing countries in Asia. In its "search for low-cost labor," NEC has begun to manufacture telephones in Thailand for export to the United States and Japan. Such an arrangement works very well for several reasons. First, the wage rate in Thailand is lower than that in Japan, Korea, Taiwan, Hong Kong, and Singapore. Second, Japanese telephone imports from Thailand tend to reduce Japan's overall trade surplus even though the telephones were made by a Japanese company and intended for Japanese use. Last, exports from NEC (in Thailand) to the United States are technically not included in the statistics of U.S. imports from Japan. This arrangement is part of NEC's "new pattern of international division of labor."

However, one suspects that the new patterns of doing business are not really new since Japan's firms invested roughly comparable amounts in both North America and Asia during the 20 years ended 1970. Also not new is the pace at which these investments have increased since 1970. As shown in Table 3.3, during the six years after 1970, Japan's firms invested over $16 billion overseas, with almost $5 billion in Asia; North America was the next largest recipient of funds at $3.8 billion.

Funds invested in Africa amounted to less than $1 billion. There was a decided investment pattern, all of which may not be explained by low-cost wages. Africa has no lack of natural resources or low-cost labor. Yet Japan's investment in developing Asia was seven times its investment in all of Africa. This discrepancy reveals another element of the Japanese psyche: racism. According to Shinto beliefs, the Japanese emperor is a direct descendant of the Japanese god. Accordingly, the average Japanese person is of lower stature and other Asians, even lower. Presumably, Caucasians are still lower, Hispanics next, and blacks, last.

Japanese contempt for blacks has been reflected in any number of public statements over time. The most recent (September 1990) was by Japanese Justice Minister Seiroku Kajiyama. Kajiyama said that prostitutes spoil a neighborhood's atmosphere "like in America when neighborhoods become mixed because blacks move in and whites are forced out." With such a perception of black people, it is not surprising that Japanese firms did not invest in Africa, but chose instead to economically colonize areas that were populated by those made more in their own image.

And invest they did. In the six years from 1977 through 1982, Japanese FDI in Asia grew by $9 billion, exceeded only by FDI of over $10 billion in North America. Thus from 1971 through 1982, Japanese direct investment in Asia totaled almost $14 billion, roughly equivalent to its investment in North America. The 1980s witnessed even higher levels of FDI. In 1989 alone, Japanese firms invested over $12 billion in Asian developing countries. Another $11 billion in loans also was provided by Japanese commercial banks during the early 1980s. By 1987, commercial loans to the region totaled $27 billion. Also in 1987, 1,583 Japanese companies operated Asian affiliates with 457,000 employees. This employment figure within Asia was roughly comparable to combined Japanese overseas employment in every other region of the world.

Thus, Japan has fueled Asian economic development with high and increasing levels of official development assistance, direct investment, loans, and employment. These catalysts along with country-specific programs for development have led to regional growth during the last 10 years or so that is unparalleled in any other region of the world.

THE RISE OF ASIA DURING THE 1980s

The decade of the 1980s may be safely considered the decade of Asia's economic ascendancy. Table 3.4 illustrates why this is an accurate description. For the eight countries shown, merchandise exports increased from $153 billion to $260 billion during the four years ended 1987, an average annual increase of 14 percent. Of these eight countries, Indonesia is the only one that posted a decline in exports. This decrease is attributable to the decline in world oil prices. Excluding petroleum products, Indonesian exports increased from $5.2 billion to $11.3 billion, an average annual increase of 21 percent.

Similarly, petroleum products are a significant part of Malaysian exports. Nonpetroleum product exports rose from $10.7 billion in 1983 to $15.4 billion, a 9.5 percent annual increase. Excluding petroleum products in Singapore's statistics, exports increased at an annual rate of 12.2 percent. As a point of reference, U.S. exports grew at a 5.4 percent rate during the same period. The acknowledged export dynamos of West Germany and Japan realized annual gains of 14.8 percent and 11.5 percent, respectively. Thus, Malaysia and Singapore experienced nonpetroleum export growth that was roughly comparable to that of Germany and Japan. Indonesia (21 percent, excluding petroleum), Thailand (16.3 percent), South Korea (17.9 percent), and Taiwan (21 percent) exceeded even these levels. Last, China, a relatively recent entrant into the capitalist realm of world trade, posted average annual gains of 21 percent.

As a result of this impressive performance, the countries' aggregate merchandise trade balance improved significantly from a deficit of $5.3 billion to a surplus of $28.3 billion. But these figures mask the role of Japan. When the trade deficits with Japan are excluded, the aggregate 1987 surplus of Korea, Singapore, Hong Kong, and Thailand grows from the official $1 billion to $19 billion. The difference, of course, represents the extent to which Japanese economic activity has been rechanneled through these four areas. Also in the same year, these countries ran an aggregate trade surplus with the United States of $22 billion, with $19 billion attributable to Hong Kong and Korea in roughly equivalent proportions. Similarly, the $19 billion trade surplus shown for Taiwan equals that country's trade balance with the United States. In other words, trade with the United States accounts for a major portion of these surpluses.

TABLE 3.4

Exports and Trade Balance of Selected Asian Countries and Territories, 1983 and 1987

(in billions of dollars)

	1983		1987	
	Exports	Trade Balance	Exports	Trade Balance
Taiwan	$ 25.1	$ 4.8	$ 53.8	$19.0
Peoples Republic of China	20.7	2.0	34.7	(1.7)
South Korea	24.4	(1.7)	47.2	6.2
Singapore	21.8	(6.3)	28.6	(3.9)
Hong Kong	22.0	(2.1)	48.5	*
Malaysia	14.1	0.9	17.9	5.3
Indonesia	18.7	1.0	17.2	4.7
Thailand	6.4	(3.9)	11.7	(1.3)
	$153.2	$(5.3)	$259.6	$28.3

*Less than $100 million.

Sources: Exports: United Nations. *Foreign Trade Statistics of Asia and the Pacific, 1983–1987.* New York: United Nations, 1989 (for South Korea, Singapore, Hong Kong, Malaysia, and Thailand); International Monetary Fund. *International Financial Statistics.* Washington, D.C.: International Monetary Fund, May 1990 (for Peoples Republic of China and Indonesia); U.S. Arms Control and Disarmament Agency. *World Military Expenditures and Arms Transfers 1988.* Washington, D.C.: U.S. Arms Control and Disarmament Agency. 1989 (for Taiwan). Trade Balances: Author's calculations based on data from the above-mentioned sources.

Not surprising, this level of trade performance has helped shift the world's balance of wealth. At the end of 1982, the seven developing countries in Asia that are shown in Table 3.5 controlled $40.6 billion in official reserves. At that time, this amount represented approximately 25 percent of the international reserves of all developing countries. Only seven years later, the seven held $151 billion, or 55 percent, of the total for developing nations. Taiwan alone held $74 billion in reserves, more than any European industrialized nation and almost as much as the United States.

When Japan is included in the analysis, the combined reserves of Japan, Taiwan, mainland China, South Korea, Singapore, Malaysia, Indonesia, and Thailand grew from $65 billion at the end of 1982 to $236 billion seven years later. Their share of the world's official international reserves jumped from 16 percent in 1982 to almost 29 percent in 1989.[3] In other words, by the end of 1989, these eight countries controlled close to one-third of the official financial resources of the entire nonsocialist world.

TABLE 3.5

International Reserves of Selected Asian Developing Nations, 1982 and
1989

	1982		1989	
	Amount(1)	%(2)	Amount(1)	%(2)
Taiwan	$ 8.7	5.3%	$ 73.8	26.7%
Peoples Republic of China	11.8	7.3	18.5	6.7
South Korea	2.8	1.7	15.2	5.5
Singapore	8.5	5.2	20.3	7.3
Malaysia	3.9	2.4	7.9	2.9
Indonesia	3.3	2.0	5.6	2.0
Thailand	1.6	(1.0)	9.6	(3.5)
	$40.6	24.9%	$150.9	54.6%
All developing countries	$162.6	100.0%	$276.5	100.0%

Notes: (1) billions of dollars; (2) percentage of total developing country international
reserves. Statistics for Hong Kong are not maintained by the International Monetary
Fund.

Sources: Amounts: International Monetary Fund. *International Financial Statistics*, May
1990. Percentages: author's calculations based on International Monetary Fund.
International Financial Statistics, May 1990.

This is not consistent with a global ebb and flow of wealth.
These changes constitute a very strong regional trend in economic
development. Further, as long as the Asian powerhouses continue to
reinvest primarily in Asia to build productive capacity and,
secondarily, in industrial countries to enhance their already
considerable technological advantages, this trend will continue.

However, this is not to suggest that there will be no significant
changes in the Asian political and economic landscape in the near term.
In fact, recent rapid changes in income and wealth set against the
backdrop of past tensions may give rise to radical political change. At
a minimum, the political changes already slated for the region suggest
rather interesting possibilities.

SINGAPORE: A CLEAR WINNER IN 1997

In 1997, Hong Kong will no longer operate as a British colony.
Instead, this stronghold of Western capitalism will become a Special
Administrative Zone of the Peoples Republic of China (PRC). The PRC
has guaranteed that Hong Kong will be permitted to continue to

transact business as it does now for another 50 years after the transition date. However, student protests in Beijing in spring 1989 led to the now infamous Tiananmen Square massacre in June of the same year. Confidence in the future autonomy of Hong Kong plummeted and the already perceptible immigration trickle from Hong Kong grew to a tidal wave. Whether or not China's intentions with respect to Hong Kong are honorable, the perception is that investments in the tiny city-state may be at risk once the Communists take over.

In terms of ease of business formation, operation, and finance, few areas in Asia appear well suited to assume the role that Hong Kong has fulfilled in recent decades. Tokyo, Seoul, and Taipei, to varying degrees, are subject to relatively strong government control. Firms that wish to invest in Japanese companies often find that their efforts are frustrated by bureaucratic and other obstacles. Long-standing ties between government and industry, long-term relationships between suppliers and manufacturers, the lifetime nature of employment, and interlocked stock ownership of keiretsu members make foreign direct investment difficult.[4]

In Korea, foreign investment over $3 million is subject to the approval of the Ministry of Finance. Not infrequently, the approval process involves approval by other industry-specific ministries. Often, this approval process results in drawn-out negotiations in which government ministries represent the interests of indigenous industry. The net effect of these negotiations is that local content of proposed products is maximized, Korean control of the venture is ensured, and technology transfer from foreign investor to Korean entity is maximized. One hundred percent foreign ownership is allowed only when the government is particularly interested in attracting the investment, usually in the area of high-technology. It should be noted that Japan has had the most success in penetrating the veil of government approval, particularly when compared with the United States.

A government approval system also exists in Taiwan. Some industries are precluded from foreign investment entirely. Examples are agricultural endeavors, national defense activities, and real estate services. In other areas, foreign investment is permitted on a restricted basis only. These categories include mining, chemical, fertilizers, pharmaceuticals, medical services, and accounting services. Here, too, high-tech investments are welcomed and encouraged, along with capital-intensive ventures.

Thus, the free-wheeling business atmosphere of Hong Kong cannot be replicated in Tokyo, Seoul, or Taipei. Given the comparatively less-developed industrial and financial systems of Malaysia, Indonesia, and Thailand, nor does it appear likely that these areas will be significant beneficiaries of capital flight from Hong Kong.

However, Singapore is a strong candidate. With a land mass of only 225 square miles, what Singapore lacks in natural resources it more than makes up for in competent government, a trained and disciplined work force, a free enterprise spirit, and social, industrial, and financial infrastructures. Subject to British colonization of one form or another after 1824 and occupied by Japan during World War II, Singapore became a self-governing state in 1959. Since independence, there has been a stable political environment and little government intervention in commercial matters.

Not unlike other Asian countries, Singapore launched an industrialization drive in the 1960s. Light manufacturing and entrepôt activities helped the economy to achieve full employment and double-digit growth. However, one of the most important elements in Singapore's growth and international prominence was the government's conscious decision to develop the financial system. Unlike the Japanese case, the financial system of Singapore was structured almost entirely using a free-enterprise model.

The Monetary Authority of Singapore (MAS) was established in 1971. During the 1960s, the government had realized that the republic's economic base would have to be broadened if it were to sustain its growth. Accordingly, the financial and banking sectors were thought to be potentially major contributors in the achievement of this goal. The charge of the MAS was, therefore, to be the central banker of the government and to foster stability of the money supply and foreign exchange conditions that would, in turn, stimulate growth within the economy. In addition, the MAS was to work to develop the financial markets in such a way that Singapore became an international financial center.

That the MAS has been successful on both fronts is a gross understatement. The steps taken have served to help Singapore become both an industrial giant and a world-class financial center. One of the features of the Singapore market is the free convertibility of the Singapore dollar. This internationally strong currency is fully backed by a basket of currencies, including the U.S. dollar, the Japanese yen, and the German mark, and gold. The Singapore dollar is freely traded without restriction. In fact, there are no foreign exchange controls in Singapore.

Another advantage that Singapore has, relative to some of its less-developed Asian counterparts, is the presence of international banks.

With twice as many foreign banks as domestic banks, Singapore has attracted financial expertise from the world over and managed to strengthen its indigenous banks in the process. When the Euromarkets began to develop, Singapore was well positioned to become one of the primary sites of the Asian dollar market, along with Hong Kong. Over 50 banks are specially licensed to conduct wholesale and offshore banking activities.

The Asian dollar market activity placed Singapore in the position of a major financial intermediary for Asia. Deposits from the Euromarket, particularly during the period of buildup of OPEC-oil-driven trade surpluses, were reinvested in Asia. Thus, in addition to capital flows from Japan, Asian dollar deposits in Singapore provided an alternative source of liquidity to the region. In the early 1980s such rechanneled funds amounted to over $13 billion.

Also favoring Singapore is its strategic location. It is an ideal trans-shipment point for Malaysia, Indonesia, Thailand, and Australia. With respect to time zones, Singapore is two hours ahead of Tokyo and 6-1/2 hours behind London, facilitating same-day telecommunications with both Asia and Europe.

Singapore's legal and financial structures and strategic location are complemented by its deliberately enforced hospitality to Western visitors. From its well-manicured and efficient airport, complete with mini-shopping mall, to its well-scrubbed streets and public facilities, to its hygienically maintained sidewalk cuisine, to the government policy encouraging politeness, English-speaking Singapore welcomes the foreign presence. Accordingly, within Asia, this city is particularly well-positioned to move to an even more prominent position in the region.

SOCIAL UNREST IN CHINA

On the other hand, future developments in China may not be as pleasant. When the PRC regains control of Hong Kong in 1997, some observers and, indeed, some residents of Hong Kong, fear that repressive measures will be instituted. Of course, such fears are rational, given the suppression of student activism in Beijing in 1989. However, a closer examination of the current relationship suggests that the worst fears probably will not be realized.

More Chinese exports are delivered to Hong Kong than to any other location, with Japan being a close second. While a substantial portion of exports that are bound for Hong Kong actually stay in Hong Kong, an equally substantial portion is re-exported. For example, in 1984, the

PRC shipped $6.6 billion of merchandise to Hong Kong (26.5 percent of total exports) and $3.6 billion represented re-exports. Re-export destinations included the United States ($1.1 billion), Japan ($273 million), Indonesia ($195 million), South Korea ($185 million), Singapore ($151 million), and Taiwan ($128 million). Shipments through Hong Kong facilitated more than $300 million in exports to South Korea and Taiwan which would, otherwise, have been more difficult, at best.

The goods that flow through Hong Kong constitute more than a quarter of China's hard currency earning capability via merchandise trade. To disrupt this arrangement would, clearly, not be in the country's best interest. Further, Hong Kong itself is an important market. China is the primary provider of foodstuffs and other primary products to Hong Kong. China has already developed effective controls to assure that price levels of these products are in line with PRC government objectives. More than 1,000 Chinese workers observe auction prices in Hong Kong in order to keep the government apprised of critical price movements. Such daily information helps Chinese officials determine the appropriate volume of exports that should be allowed. These monitoring exercises already give China a large measure of control over the Hong Kong market. Strong-arm tactics would appear to have marginal benefit.

In addition to its functions as a trans-shipment facility and final export market, Hong Kong is also the home of a vital branch of the Bank of China and 12 other Chinese state-owned banks. These banks help finance Chinese imports and exports. In addition, the Bank of China is a listening post for the government's gathering of intelligence with respect to developments in the Western world. Disrupting the status quo in Hong Kong would also disrupt these processes.

Clearly, the PRC has many motivations to allow Hong Kong to conduct its business as usual. It appears that a more likely source of unrest after 1997 may be the mainland Chinese. After all, 1988 per capita GNP in Hong Kong was $9,230 but only $330 on the mainland. Once Hong Kong is officially a part of China, the income disparity may fuel civil disorder that the central government could have difficulty controlling.

Several factors suggest such a scenario. First, Chinese people have a strong cultural and ideological foundation. They always have been more culturally advanced than the rest of Asia, indeed, a good deal more than the rest of the world. Chinese art is the oldest known to man and the written form of the Japanese language is derived from Chinese ideograms. In turn, Chinese ideograms are believed to have originated in the period from 1523 to 1027 B.C., along with the first Chinese cities.

In more recent times, grass-roots activism has been a standard part of Chinese society. After the Taiping Rebellion from 1850 through 1864, instigated by a radical military-religious movement, guilds, neighborhood associations, and religious groups stepped in to meet pressing social needs. These organizations provided relief for the poor, maintained order, and led water conservation efforts. Such groups were formalized in 1903 as chambers of commerce, bankers associations, and lawyers associations. While the government gave them their official designations, it was the social group that they each represented that gave them their real political power.

Through such groups lively discussion of political issues has become commonplace at the local level. A kind of self-regulation is, therefore, encouraged through active dialogue of relevant issues.

At the same time, the open-door policies established by the central government have promised much and delivered relatively little. The stated objectives were efficient resource allocation, technological modernization, establishment of a base for sustained economic growth, and improvement in the standard of living for Chinese people. The direction of change was to be toward greater decentralization of microeconomic decision making, greater market orientation (vis-à-vis central planning), and increased foreign trade, investment, and technology. Understandably, expectations were raised.

Agricultural reforms have enabled farmers to lease land for as long as 15 to 20 years and to sell a portion of output at market prices. Response was quick and dramatic. Grain output grew from 305 million metric tons in 1978 to 407 million in 1984.

Industrial reform has made it possible for state enterprises to retain part of their profits for new investment, worker bonuses, and welfare benefits and to have more control over production decisions. Above-quota output can be sold at market prices. However, any additional investment funds must be raised in financial markets, that is, must meet profitability criteria. In addition, collective and individual enterprises have been encouraged and are currently the fastest-growing segments of Chinese industry.

However, very real problems persist. It is estimated that there are over 260 million surplus rural workers. The number of farmers in China is said to approach 800 million. In contrast, the United States has 3.5 to 4 million farmers. Ignoring this excess rural population, China must create 15 million new jobs a year just to accommodate population growth. With a total annual government budget of $78 billion, there are scarce resources to seriously address these pressing social needs.

The combination of high, unmet expectations and a strong grass-roots tradition has led to increased regionalism within China. The austerity measures introduced to cool inflation in 1988 have been met with minimal acceptance. Even party representatives at the provincial level are increasingly in disagreement with the central government.

Further, it will be difficult, indeed, for the central government to rein in the forces that are gaining momentum. Already, by its own admission, the Ministry of Finance has control of not much more than one-half of the total money in circulation. As much as 40 percent of currency is being hoarded. Further, the 18 million new, nonstate-owned enterprises employ 90 million people.

When Hong Kong is brought under PRC control, resistance to recentralization efforts may be enough to spark civil disorder. An activist, ambitious, market-oriented Chinese populace may find the income inequities more than it can tolerate.

WILL TAIWAN BE THE ANSWER?

The central government of the PR will realize, at some point, that the current pace of economic change is unacceptable. It also will realize that its dwindling control over both the money supply and productive enterprises will be insufficient to effect more significant change. Nevertheless, it appears unlikely that a new direction in leadership will emerge from the old guard. Elder, Soviet-trained party leaders are ill-equipped to devise and execute an adequate economic strategy. The September 1988 decision to recentralize is an example. In response to high inflation due, at least partially, to new agricultural and industrial profitability and resulting higher cash balances in the hands of the private sector, the central government decided to attempt to reduce economic opportunity through an austerity and recentralization program.

Capitalist expansion cannot be achieved through a series of starts and stops. A more constructive approach would have been to provide productive outlets for the hoarded cash, not ask the new entrepreneurs to give the excess back to the government to manage.

The central government of the PRC will eventually realize that foreign investment must be more actively encouraged. Up to this point, the central government has been lukewarm unless the FDI was high-tech or export-oriented. Further, the government has resisted the management and labor training and other organizational aspects of foreign economic presence. To date, the majority of foreign firms have been more interested in selling to the Chinese domestic market. The PRC has competitive disadvantages with respect to training and discipline of work force, transportation, communications, and relative freedom from government intervention. The fact is that China will benefit from foreign investment whenever its people receive training, investment opportunities, and/or the possibility of acting as suppliers to the new establishments.

However, it appears that only a Western-style leader will be capable of coming to these fundamental conclusions. Perhaps, such a leader will come from the ranks of the student demonstrators in Tiananmen Square. In the meantime, the PRC will continue to face significant economic challenges.

In fact, the challenges may lead to collective desperation by the central government. In such a state, usurping the power of the Nationalist government in Taiwan may appear to be an expedient means to a desirable end. Hong Kong has been a very useful contact point with the Western world. Further, the capitalist activities of the Bank of China have not contaminated the People's Republic. If Taiwan were also a Special Administrative Zone, the hard currency potential would be considerable.

Rather substantial financial flows already originate from the small island nation. Hong Kong re-exports from China to Taiwan increase each year. In 1988, 430,000 Chinese from Taiwan visited the PRC carrying an average of $5,000 each in gifts or money. This represents over $2 billion of unofficial aid in 1988 alone. If Taiwan were a Special Administrative Zone, its trade surpluses would potentially make an additional $20 billion in investment funds available to the mainland. As of 1985, 85 percent of the value of Chinese FDI originated from Hong Kong, its soon-to-be Special Administrative Zone. Of course, the $70 billion in Taiwanese international reserves could be put to productive use as well.

There are already some indications that the PRC would not be averse to a reconciliation with the Nationalist government. Officially, China considers Taiwan a province, not an independent country. The PRC has designated four coastal locations as Special Economic Zones (SEZs): Shantou, Shenzhen, Xiamen, and Zhuhai. All four are in areas from which most of the overseas Chinese immigrated. Accordingly, the residents of the SEZs and the overseas Chinese speak the same dialect. Two of the four (Shantou and Xiamen) are directly across the Formosa Strait, no more than 200 miles away.

The purpose of Special Economic Zones is to attract foreign investment for export activity while keeping the domestic economy insulated. Special permission is required to sell SEZ output in the rest of China, but investments for export industries are exempt from income taxation and land-use fees for up to ten years. Further, specific categories of SEZ production, especially in Shantou and Xiamen, are exempt from export duties. Extending the SEZ concept to the entire island of Taiwan is a relatively short leap in logic.

Of course, this development depends upon the military supremacy of the PRC over Taiwan because, clearly, China needs Taiwan more than Taiwan needs China. However, this supremacy is questionable. While China's submarine, nuclear-missile, and satellite programs meet high quality standards, aircraft engine design and military electronics are less impressive.

Even more importantly, the efforts aimed at military modernization that began in the late 1970s have had deleterious effects on morale. Among the objectives were streamlining and professionalizing military personnel. One million active personnel were "demobilized," primarily senior officers. Unfortunately, in many cases there were no civilian jobs waiting for them, causing some to resort to criminal activity in order to survive. Those that remained often were subject to reassignment as military units were merged. Breaking up established networks of loyalty bred mistrust of the new arrangements.

Presumably, the streamlining was to make room for younger, better-educated officers. However, the young rural male found that he could better advance his financial condition by staying at home and working in the new, market-oriented agricultural sector. As an added inducement, he also was able to marry and start a family. Draft evasion became commonplace. Likewise, the more-educated urban youth, that the central government had hoped would form the core of the new, more-sophisticated military, generally chose to remain unemployed rather than to join. Those urban youth that did sign up were not well received by military officers, who felt the urban youngsters were not rugged enough or that they might pose disciplinary problems.

These recruiting problems have been solved, in many cases, by military raids on homes where draft-age young men have been known to reside and by induction of socially and physically unfit individuals. The result is that the Chinese military is now full of mistrustful, unfit, and unwilling participants.

Since there exists some doubt that this restructured military will follow a straight party line in every instance, China may not be able to convince Taiwan to cooperate and become a second Special Administrative Zone. In fact, if the PRC does not make the proper adjustments to encourage foreign investment and domestic industrialization, the central government may find that it has, indeed, lost its legitimacy. In such an event, it may be the Nationalist government that is once again seated in Beijing.

THE TROUBLED REUNIFICATION OF KOREA

In this era of superpower reconciliation, EC harmonization, and German reunification, the reunification of Korea is a distinct possibility. At the time of this writing, the merging of East and West has not yet led to serious disruptions of the German industrial or financial sectors. Even the $200 billion conversion of East German currency to Deutsche marks (DMs) caused hardly a ripple in the international value of the DM. At least on the surface, smooth absorption of the East German work force and the provision of adequate housing and social services appear to be the most challenging aspects of the merger. However, in Korea, the weight of the North will create a much more severe burden for the South. A comparative analysis of the Korean situation vis-à-vis the German suggests that the Korean transition will be neither smooth nor painless.

In terms of *population*, South Korea will have to absorb a relatively greater number of former Communists. The 61 million West Germans outnumbered the less than 17 million East Germans by a ratio of 3.7 to 1. In Korea, the South to North ratio of 43 million to 22 million is only 1.9 to 1. Thus, during the economic adjustment phase, every North Korean will be supported by less than two South Koreans, while each former East German has almost four capitalist counterparts.

The two cases are also different in terms of trends in population growth. The West German population declined at the rate of 0.1 percent from 1980 to 1988, while South Korea's grew 1.4 percent per year. West Germany needed a boost in its labor force. South Korea has no such void. In fact, recent Korean moves toward democratization have inspired labor unrest and demands for higher wages and benefits. As a result, in 1987 and 1988, wages increased by 17 percent and 14 percent, respectively. A significant increase in the labor pool will generate an incentive for South Korean industry to decrease wages. Clearly, the potential for further conflict exists.

If the *pattern of migration* in the German case is indicative of that which would develop in Korea, the new members of the Korean family will head for the cities. This will create an additional strain on the infrastructures of host cities. In the early 1980s, Korean urban populations grew at an average annual rate of 4.2 percent, while the urban populations of Germany grew at only 0.1 percent. Even so, German reunification migration has placed real pressure on urban capacity. The pressure will be even greater in Korea.

Further, urban population is not similarly distributed in the two countries. In the early 1980s, 41 percent of Korea's urban population lived in Seoul, the nation's largest city. In contrast, only 18 percent of West Germany's population resided in West Berlin. While 11 West German cities had a population of 500,000 or more, only seven South Korean cities did so. Fully 77 percent of urban population lived in those seven Korean cities. The 11 large German cities housed only 45 percent of that country's urbanites.

Simply stated, South Korean cities already are more densely populated than West German cities. In fact, the whole country is more densely populated. The total number of South Korean residents is 70 percent of the total number of West Germans. Yet, South Koreans occupy only 40 percent of the land mass of West Germany.

Such demographic imbalances conceivably could be overcome if the *industrial sector* were poised to absorb new entrants into the capitalist world of South Korea. Unfortunately, this does not appear to be the case.

Korean growth, like German growth, has been fueled by *export activity*. During the 1980s, South Korean exports increased faster than German overseas shipments.[5] In 1977, Korea exported 8.5 percent as much as Germany. By 1989, the Korean percentage had grown to over 18 percent of German exports. However, with population equalling that of 70 percent of West Germany, South Korea's export productivity still lags significantly behind Germany's.

The analysis of export productivity is even less favorable when North Korea is compared to East Germany. The North Korean population is 31 percent larger than the East German. While the latter exported merchandise valued at $31 billion in 1987, the former exported only $1.7 billion. The absorption of North Koreans may prove to be a significant challenge for South Korean export industries.

These differences in relative export activity are reflected in comparative *income levels*. In 1987, per capita GNP for East and West Germany was roughly $9,200 and $14,000, respectively. In the same year, comparable figures for North and South Korea were $1,200 and $2,700, respectively. South Korea is still a developing country. West Germany is a mature, fully industrialized nation. Even South Korean international reserves, which more than quadrupled to $15 billion during the seven years ended 1989, pale in comparison to West Germany's $65 billion. South Korea's external debt of $31 billion serves to further compound its relatively weaker financial position.[6]

Thus, it appears exceedingly likely that Korean reunification will cause chaotic upheaval. The new union will need to boost production and exports. Its most important export industries are electronics and textiles. However, on both fronts, the country faces growing resistance in its largest market, the United States. (By comparison, Japanese and EC markets are not as open to Korean exports.) Americans may not respond sympathetically to the needs of the new Korea since many will still have vivid memories of U.S. plant closings in both the textiles and electronics industries. Besides, the U.S. government has little, if any, discretionary funds for foreign aid.

Korea will be forced to turn to Japan. Actually, this will be more of a swerve than a turn. In 1987, Korea received one-third of its imports from Japan, up from less than one-quarter just four years earlier. While the United States is Korea's largest export market, Japan is its second most important. The trade ties, therefore, already exist. As noted earlier in the chapter, Japan also has channeled official assistance and direct investment into the South Korean economy. With such a large stake in the region, Japan will respond.

However, there will be little altruism in this Korean rescue effort. Japan will extract economic concessions from Korea the likes of which have not been seen since the peninsula was invaded at the turn of the century and subsequently annexed.

With its newly established crude oil sources in place in China and the Soviet Union, Japan may very well require Korea to modify, as necessary, its underutilized petrochemical capacity in order to start refining the crude. The coal in North Korea also will move Japan closer to its energy goals, particularly if its early 1980s investments in Chinese coal mines are productive.[7]

The iron ore in North Korea probably will be mined by the decidedly cheap labor there and processed in South Korean steel mills, currently the most efficient in the world. Procuring high-quality chromium steel at concessionary prices for automobile and truck manufacture would give Japan an even greater advantage in the auto industry.

The cheap labor of the northern regions of Korea will be ideally suited for Japan's strategy of "global division of labor." Textiles and electronic-chip assembly operations would reduce transportation costs associated with more distant locations. Further, Japan may import some of Korea's excess labor since it faces a fairly acute labor shortage because of its aging work force.

The Korean government should, generally, be willing to give Japan what it desires in terms of control over mineral deposits and production facilities. There will be no alternative. As it is, the "chaebol," Korean counterparts of the Japanese keiretsus currently employ a relatively small share of Korean workers. For example, while there were 700 Korean electronics firms in 1983, only three accounted for 40 percent of electronics exports and production. The remaining firms were small contractors and suppliers for the larger firms. The high percentage of small (in some cases, sweat-shop) operations suggests that significant job creation will have to originate from outside investment and assistance. South Korea may receive from Japan the high-technology investment that it has sought for many years, albeit on not particularly favorable terms.

THE POTENTIALLY TURBULENT 1990s

The 1980s constituted the decade of economic ascendancy for Asia. Its star probably will continue to rise. However, rapid change, even favorable change, carries with it certain stresses. These stresses may be relieved through intraregional adjustments that end up being just as dramatic as the region's meteoric economic advances. Perhaps, the 1990s will come to be referred to as the decade of Asia's political realignment.

NOTES

1. In all cases, money paid within the region has not been directed to those recipients originally intended. That is, there has been a certain amount of corruption in Asia with respect to Japanese payments. However, unlike the U.S./Central American situation, Japan has not demanded that recipients espouse democracy or maintain an environment free of corruption. Instead, Japan has demanded only specified results for its corporate sector.

2. Again, this also has been true of developing countries located close to the United States. The difference in the two situations is that U.S. labor unions have fought U.S. corporate expansion into these areas by referring to Mexican and other labor as *slave labor*. This appears to be only a smoke screen, however, since other areas are not subjected to the same test. For example, an athlete in the National Basketball Association (NBA) may earn $4 million a year. His counterpart in the

Canadian league may earn only one-hundredth of that amount. There is never an outcry that the Canadian athlete is working for slave wages. Similar analogies can be drawn between hourly workers and senior management.

3.   This analysis excludes socialist countries for which information about international reserves is not available to the public through the International Monetary Fund, United Nations, or World Bank.

4.   As explained in Chapter 2, with the low level of pension benefits, the lifetime job is more akin to lifetime exploitation.

5.   From 1980 through 1987, West German and South Korean exports grew at real annual rates of 4.7 percent and 14.3 percent, respectively.

6.   South Korean debt peaked at $47 billion in 1985. Since that time, the government has reduced the balance outstanding each year.

7.   Japan would rather depend on Asian countries for energy needs. Energy producers in the Middle East are not as easily controlled.

4

European Community 1992: The United States of Europe

THE ROUGH ROAD TO UNITY

December 31, 1992, will mark an important milestone in the economic evolution of Western Europe.[1] By that date, the 12 members of the European Community (EC) will have effected a single European market. This is not an initiative intended to globalize these markets. It is, instead, an attempt to create the United States of Europe, a strong regional trading block.

However, because of past hostilities among EC members, the challenges of East European development, and pressure from Asian competition, achievement of the ultimate goal will not be an easy task. Specifically,

1. The EC negotiation for a single market will be characterized by secret agreements and sideline deal making.
2. The United Kingdom may emerge as the most economically powerful EC member because Germany will be fully committed to and preoccupied by revitalization of what was East Germany and other former Soviet satellites.
3. The reconstruction of Eastern Europe will place a heavy burden on the former West Germany, one which other EC members will be less than anxious to help carry.
4. Nontraditional market mechanisms will evolve to provide outlets for East European goods, some involving barter with resource-rich African countries that have been virtually ignored for the past 30 years.

5. The Japanese may exploit the German vulnerability that is created by this enormous social responsibility, causing competition in world markets between the two countries to become increasingly vicious.
6. To gain access to the low-cost labor pool in Eastern Europe and, at the same time, avoid attendant reconstruction costs, Japanese firms will shift investment activity from the United States to Germany. Targets are likely to be those German enterprises that have paved the way into Eastern Europe and identified the most promising ventures, but may lack investment capital in the environment of a newly overextended Germany.

THE EUROPEAN COMMUNITY: STRANGE BEDFELLOWS

In 1985, the 12 countries of the EC announced plans to effect a Single European Market by December 31, 1992. The origins of this concept date back to the 1957 Treaty of Rome among six countries that created the European Economic Community (EEC), also referred to as the Common Market.[2] EEC members sought to coordinate monetary policies and actions for their mutual benefit. The 1967 amalgamation of the EEC with two other European industrial associations gave birth to the European Community (EC) as it is known today.[3]

A 1970 report to the EC (the Werner Report) recommended that EC members pool their reserves and settle trade balances internally, that they maintain their exchange rates within predetermined parities, and that eventually all national currencies be replaced by one Community currency.[4] The European Monetary System (EMS) emerged in 1979, largely out of the Werner Report recommendations. One of the key provisions was the creation of the European Currency Unit (ECU), a basket of European currencies to settle central bank obligations.[5] The European Monetary Fund would issue the ECUs against member deposits of gold and foreign currency and all exchange rate parities were respecified in terms of the ECU.

The decision in 1985 to create a Single European Market called for removal of most barriers to trade and capital flow. Accordingly, EC directives have been issued in areas from government purchasing to intellectual property rights to environmental protection to financial services. The idea is that the legal framework for doing business in Europe should not vary from one country to the next.

Theoretically, this appears to be a feasible undertaking, at least on the surface. However, for centuries European countries have fought for regional dominance. As early as the sixteenth century, Spain, enriched by the gold and silver that it had stolen from the newly conquered Americas, attempted to overtake Britain. Britain repelled the attack and went on to establish its own empire in the New World. Then in rivalry with France, Britain fought a seven-year war (ending in 1763) that resulted in the loss of French territories in North America and India.

France received partial vindication when it supported the colonies during the American Revolution, contributing to the decline of the first British Empire. Now a hotbed of social debate, France exported internal conflict to the rest of Europe from 1792 through 1802 during the French Revolution. Fighting broke out again only a year later when Britain precipitated the Napoleonic Wars (1803–1815) that brought military confrontation to much of Europe before the French defeat at Waterloo.

Germany began to assert its desire for regional dominance in the late 1800s. The Austro-Prussian (1866) and Franco-Prussian (1870–1871) Wars served to consolidate the German empire. The German desire to assert its will over the rest of the continent contributed to World War I (1914–1918) and that country's defeat. Punishing war reparations, hyperinflation, and the Great Depression created a favorable environment in Germany for the rise of Adolph Hitler. France and Britain first appeased Hitler's expansionary tendencies by handing over a part of Czechoslovakia. However, when Hitler's forces invaded Poland, the two countries immediately declared war on Germany. The participants in World War II would include the United States and virtually all of Europe, Asia, and the South Pacific. The end of the war in 1945 marked the beginning of the painful process of reconstruction.

The old adversaries in the new Western Europe presumably would coexist peacefully. Concerns for economic well-being have replaced threats of military aggression. However, the few years since World War II do not appear to be sufficient to counteract all the old animosities and nationalist tendencies.

POLITICAL AND ECONOMIC INFIGHTING

Each country will continue to position itself to serve its own best interests, before and after 1992. There are a number of examples to illustrate these dynamics.

Former Prime Minister Margaret Thatcher attempted to slow down the pace of monetary union for many years, citing the importance of sovereign control over the money supply. The French president of the Executive Commission, Jacques Delores, has been one of the strongest advocates of the monetary union and federalism in general.[6] Their differing opinions were motivated by nationalist concerns.

During the 1980s, the Thatcher government took strong measures to make the United Kingdom more competitive. State-owned enterprises were privatized, the fiscal deficit was reduced every year and became a surplus in 1989, and financial markets were liberalized during the Big Bang of 1986 to encourage foreign investment. The large trade deficits that plagued the country were largely attributable to the importation of capital goods to help make industry more efficient. All the while, tight control of the money supply was used to fight inflation. As a restructured world financial center, the United Kingdom may not be well served if it must relinquish control of its currency.

On the other hand, France has had much less success with the free-market model. In France, perhaps the most centrally planned economy in the industrialized West, large firms and monopolies have not been uncommon. After the first oil shock in 1973, however, the central planning process was relaxed to allow a greater flow of funds to those industries that the government wished to encourage. While exports improved, the experience was, essentially, that French entrepreneurs did not reinvest in the industrial infrastructure of the country. Instead, they opted for real estate developments in the south of France or, worse yet, foreign investments with no benefit to the French. When socialists took over in 1981, greater state control was reinstituted.

The socialists hoped that they could manage the more efficient, free-market firms to accomplish their stated agenda. However, they found over half of the firms in financial distress. It was not until after 1985 that the government was able to restore the ailing companies to solvency. Since then, price controls have been reduced, credit controls abolished, and financial markets modernized. A strong European central bank and a unified currency will only extend the benefits of French central planning. Such developments would be in the best interest of France.

Thus, there has been a built-in philosophical difference between the governments of the United Kingdom and France. Italy aligned itself with France on this matter for even more pressing nationalist reasons. Italy struggles with an economy that is severely polarized. The industrial North is an efficient high-income region, while the South is poorly managed and lacks basic infrastructure in many cases. Organized crime in the South and corruption in central government have, collectively, squandered the more than $300 billion earmarked to develop the South over the last few decades. The situation is a financial drain on the country. A strong EC currency could only help.

At the other end of the spectrum is Germany. Until recently, the Germans had strong reservations about the monetary union and feared that a "hard" ECU would be an unsatisfactory substitute for the Deutsche mark. At least in this regard, the Germans agreed with the English.

However, these objectives suddenly evaporated in October 1990, when German Chancellor Helmut Kohl proposed a compromise date of January 1, 1994, as the deadline for laying the foundation of a European central bank. In an unexpected development, Italian Prime Minister Giulio Andreotti pushed through a commitment to the 1994 date and the hard ECU (by 1997) during the EC summit a few days after the announcement of Kohl's proposed compromise date. The United Kingdom was left to object alone, having not expected the issue to be addressed until the group's December meeting. Kohl had acquiesced, presumably after being assured by Andreotti that the European central bank would be independent of government control (as is the Bundesbank) and that it would not be permitted to issue money to accommodate fiscal deficits of member countries.

However, one is left to wonder whether the change of heart had more to do with behind-the-scenes negotiations. Interestingly, during the same month, Kohl signed a friendship treaty with the Soviet Union to accommodate the reunification effort. As a result, there were complaints that Germany was molding unilateral foreign policy, violating the spirit of multilateral European policy. Undaunted by these complaints, Kohl negotiated a NATO proposal with the United States.[7] The proposal included the use of nuclear weapons in defense against the Soviet Union in the event of a crisis that could not be resolved through more conservative means. Since his own foreign minister advised against inclusion of a nuclear alternative, Kohl must have had some reason to believe that the other EC members would not object.

Could it be that these issues were broached and settled during Kohl's private meetings with French President François Mitterrand (September) and Italian Prime Minister Giulio Andreotti (October)? Could the exchange have been monetary union for political/military concessions? Whatever the true dynamics, the struggle for power and national interests will play no insignificant role in the evolution of the United States of Europe.

THE UNITED KINGDOM: POISED FOR GROWTH

The decade of Thatcher's rule as prime minister was marked by the transformation of the British economy from one that had been heavily laden with increasing social expenditures and poor productivity gains to one that, by 1988, expanded at a rate second only to Japan in the industrialized West.

The change began in 1975 with a recognition that export-led growth probably would be more sustainable than stimulation through fiscal deficits. Wages had been pegged to inflation. After the oil crisis of 1973 (and before North Sea reserves had been exploited), these pegged wages increased by 50 percent during the two years ended 1975. With this kind of inflation, foreign holders of sterling sold heavily. Between March 1975 and September 1976, official reserves dropped by almost $3 billion as authorities sold foreign currency to break the fall of the pound. By the end of 1976, official reserves stood at a record low of $3.4 billion.

In 1977, the United Kingdom announced to the International Monetary Fund that the government would limit both its borrowing and the expansion of credit in the economy. In addition, government expenditures would be reduced and imports limited. When the expected trade deficit was actually a small surplus, capital flow into the United Kingdom picked up once again. Starting in 1976, North Sea oil began to substitute for imported crude, further improving the country's trade picture over time.

In 1979, the Thatcher government began opening the economy to free-market forces. The emphasis has been on privatizing state-run industries and eliminating redundant capacity. Public spending increased at a slower rate than revenues so that the 1983 budget deficit of £13.4 billion was reduced to £3.2 billion by 1987. In 1989, the unemployment rate was at its lowest level in ten years and the fiscal budget was in surplus. The negative aspects of the U.K. economy over this period were that the savings rate had dropped and the merchandise trade balance had steadily worsened to a deficit of $37 billion by 1988 (about 4.4 percent of GNP).

From 1983 through 1988, exports in the United Kingdom grew at an average annual rate of over 9 percent in U.S. dollar terms or at roughly 6 percent in sterling terms.[8] However, imports grew even faster — 14 percent in dollar terms or 10 percent in sterling terms.

The United States also has run large trade deficits in recent years. While exports over the same period grew at almost 10 percent, imports grew at almost 11 percent. However, there is a substantial difference between the two countries in the manner in which government finance has been managed. The United Kingdom brought its fiscal budget into surplus even as unemployment was being reduced. The U.S. experience has been a large, stubborn, and now increasing fiscal deficit.

Another important distinction between the two countries is the level of business investment. A high level of imports can reflect high consumption demand, high investment demand, or a combination of the two. Investment demand generally will be tied to higher future output and productivity. As seen in Table 4.1, business investment in the United Kingdom increased over 14 percent in real terms in 1987. This was the highest among those industrialized countries shown, including Japan and West Germany. In the United States, business investment increased less than 4 percent. In 1988, U.K. investment increases topped 20 percent, as U.S. firms showed only an 8 percent increase. In 1989, U.K. gains in investment activity fell back to 7 percent. However, this was still twice the U.S. rate.

Thus, trade deficits in themselves are not necessarily signs of trouble. Quite the contrary, when government finance is being handled wisely and capital investment is high, such deficits can be a precursor to subsequent economic expansion. Indeed, this has been the case in Asia as was illustrated in Chapters 2 and 3.

Further, it is not inconceivable that the United Kingdom has learned several valuable lessons from present and former colonies in the Pacific Rim. With far fewer natural resources than its British parent, Hong Kong has moved to the forefront of world economics by exporting a full range of manufactured goods to the rest of the world at competitive prices. This principle can also work for the United Kingdom. The above-mentioned industrial restructuring, together with the country's well-educated work force and long tradition in manufacturing, give the United Kingdom a strong competitive edge in a number of industries.

While the changes of the past decade have positioned the country for future growth, certain immediate problems must be addressed.

TABLE 4.1
Business Investment in Selected Industrialized Countries, 1987–1989
(annual % change)

	1987	1988	1989
Canada	11.1%	18.9%	8.2%
United States	3.9	8.4	3.4
Japan	8.2	15.5	17.8
France	4.8	10.5	4.9
West Germany	4.2	7.3	8.6
Italy	10.4	11.2	6.7
United Kingdom	14.2	20.2	7.0

Source: International Monetary Fund. *World Economic Outlook*, May 1990, p. 6.

Because of the high level of economic activity, the rate of inflation went from a low of 2 percent in 1986 to 11 percent in 1990. The government's tight money policy, intended to control inflation, brought a slowdown in the economy in 1990. Companies experienced greater difficulty in arranging financing through their banks, a number of large industrial firms failed, and unemployment began to creep upward.

Under these circumstances, the United Kingdom may find it necessary to do more than use Hong Kong as an example for economic growth. As the 1997 expiration of the British lease approaches, the United Kingdom may be well advised to offer incentives to those Hong Kong enterprises that are seeking a new home. Should the central government of China continue to attempt to exert the level of control over individual freedoms that became common after the 1989 Tiananmen Square incident, incentives may not be necessary.

Whatever precipitates such transplanting of Hong Kong companies, the subsequent cultural transition would be fairly easy. The British have long-standing business relationships with the overseas Chinese of Hong Kong, as well as an appreciation of their culture. Business in Hong Kong is transacted in English (although some knowledge of Cantonese is useful). Geographically, both Hong Kong and the United Kingdom are island states. In many ways, it is a natural match.

Another useful precedent for the United Kingdom is its former colony of Singapore. In 1970, Singapore decided to complement its industrial base by encouraging the growth of international banking and finance. This objective clearly has been achieved. During the 1970s, the United Kingdom protected British domestic money supply and financial system from outside influence by restricting nonresident transactions in sterling and foreign ownership of domestic financial institutions. At the same time, the Eurodollar market was permitted to flourish, as London fulfilled the function of an offshore financial center for U.S. dollar transactions.

One of the first official acts of the Thatcher government in 1979 was to remove sterling exchange controls and to encourage more competition among domestic financial institutions. The Big Bang of 1986 opened these same institutions to foreign ownership. While such liberalization is part of the overall harmonization goals of the EC, London has a competitive advantage because of its centuries-old tradition of international finance.

There appears to be a consensus that the freedom of consumption and investment funds to flow cross-border will be one of the most pronounced benefits of the Single European Market. An opinion poll on this topic was conducted throughout the EC during 1988. Respondents

TABLE 4.2
Foreign Liabilities of EC Domestic Banks, Third Quarter 1989

	Amount (1)	% (2)
Belgium	$ 194.3	3.4%
Denmark	25.8(3)	0.5
France	332.0	5.9
Germany	143.4	2.5
Greece	13.1	0.2
Ireland	11.9	0.2
Italy	117.1(4)	2.1
Luxembourg	224.8	4.0
Netherlands	120.8	2.1
Spain	42.6	0.8
United Kingdom	$1,000.4	17.7
All countries	$5,640.1	100.0%

Notes: (1) billions of U.S. dollars; (2) percentage of the total foreign liabilities of all countries; (3) balance as of 1988 (third quarter); (4) balance as of 1988 (fourth quarter). Information for Portugal was not available. However, the 1986 balance was less than $2 billion.

Sources: Amounts: International Monetary Fund. *International Financial Statistics,* May 1990, p. 52; Percentages, author's calculations based on International Monetary Fund. *International Financial Statistics,* May 1990, p. 52.

were asked to classify the post-1992 freedom of circulation of specific goods and services as either an advantage or disadvantage. On average, the increased ease of making payments and carrying money ranked highest as advantages of the Single European Market.

The United Kingdom controls more foreign deposits than any other EC country. As shown in Table 4.2, these deposits amounted to $1 trillion in 1989, or over 17 percent of the world total.[9] France held the next highest concentration among EC members with $332 billion or just under 6 percent of the world total.

Clearly, experience in and capacity for international financial services can only serve to complement cost-efficient industrial infrastructure. These will be the keys to economic expansion in post-1992 Europe. The United Kingdom has both.

GERMANY: CARRYING THE WEIGHT OF EASTERN EUROPE

The competitive advantages of the United Kingdom notwithstanding, conventional wisdom often gives Germany the edge in a unified Europe. However, the financial drain of restructuring former

Soviet satellites may prove to be more taxing than the Germans originally anticipated.

It should be noted that the Germans are not interested in opening up the East purely for humanitarian reasons any more than the Japanese intended to raise the standard of living in the four Asian newly industrialized countries (NICs).[10] The Germans hope to capitalize on low-cost labor, just as the Japanese have done in their cross-border expansion. Territories that could not be held through military aggression may now be colonized through economic domination. However, the similarities end there.

The needs throughout Eastern Europe are large and varied. Housing, industrial infrastructure, and the environment have all suffered from over 50 years of neglect. Further, the ability of the region to borrow its way out of this predicament is limited in several cases by already-high debt levels.

East Germans historically have maintained the highest standard of living among East Europeans and were the most Westernized and modernized. Nevertheless, a comparison between East Germany and the rest of Europe yields dramatic contrasts. More than three-quarters of the population lives in dwellings constructed before 1945 and half of these before 1914. There has been virtually no investment in industry to produce consumer durable goods or in the public sector to develop adequate transportation and telecommunication systems. Worse yet, the process of central planning has rendered the whole economy inflexible with little inherent ability to adapt to rapidly changing conditions. Past centralized decision making isolated East Germany from the rest of the world, making it impossible for the country to develop competitively.

Indeed, mismanagement of people and resources did serious internal damage to both. The highly regulated labor market discouraged excellence and initiative. Unable to move freely from one job to another, a worker's individual strengths were unlikely to be developed. In the absence of competition, few competitive advantages will surface.

Under the Soviet version of Communism, citizens were taught to let the central government make decisions and take initiatives. "Free enterprise" had no meaning. Such attitudes became the standard of behavior. This was not the case in developing Asian countries in which Japan has had a major economic role. Hard work and free enterprise in Hong Kong and Singapore have been the watchwords for decades. Even in the more controlled economies of South Korea and Taiwan, high productivity has long been a valued concept.

China, the major communist force in Asia, has consistently experimented with capitalism since the 1949 change of government. The Bank of China maintains Westernized branches in overseas locations including Hong Kong, London, and New York. The domestic agricultural banking system has operated in a cooperative system with regional branches raising funds through local deposits, that is, farmers financing themselves. Cooperatives and individuals have had the right to sell goods and services in free market mechanisms beginning in 1979. While Japan was not required to instill a work ethic in other Asians, Germany will not be so fortunate.

While individual initiative was stifled, the East European environment was exploited. The central decision to rely heavily on lignite (brown coal), accompanied by no emphasis on energy efficiency, has led to severe air pollution. East Germany is currently the world's largest producer of carbon dioxide. Homes are covered by soot and motorists often must use headlights during the day.

As critical as the East German environmental situation is, it is better than the condition of other East European countries. In Hungary, the water in the Danube River is black because of the high content of industrial and municipal wastes. Lead poisoning is a threat in Poland, where vegetables and fruit contain ten times the level of lead that is considered safe by United Nations standards. Reversing the effects of past pollution in Eastern Europe may cost billions of dollars. The cost of transforming industry so that it is more environmentally compatible will add additional billions to the cost of environmental protection.

In the case of Asian developing countries, their environment was not seriously threatened before Japanese firms began their expansion drive. A multibillion dollar cleanup was not required in the formative stages of their economic development.

The tab for other infrastructural overhauls in Eastern Europe bring the estimates for modernization to staggering levels. For example, updating the transportation system in East Germany alone could require over $100 billion. Needed telecommunications improvements throughout the region could cost $350 billion over 15 years.

Borrowing the necessary funds seems improbable, given the already-high external debt level of approximately $100 billion in the aggregate.[11] For the two most heavily debt-laden countries, Poland and Hungary, 1989 external debt was on the order of 65 percent of gross national product. For the entire developing region of Europe and the Mediterranean, 1988 debt was somewhat lower at 44 percent of GNP.[12]

In contrast, developing-country debt in East Asia and the Pacific was only 27 percent of 1988 GNP.[13] In 1980, before the NICs had attained their current economic status, debt was only 17 percent of GNP. Thus, comparing the debt levels of Asian countries in 1980, when several of them were beginning to have a significant impact on world markets, to 1988 debt levels in Eastern Europe, where only a few had started to make market inroads, one notes that European debt was more than 2-1/2 times as high as Asian debt.[14]

With somewhat limited debt capacity and minimal internal sources of capital, Eastern Europe must hope for a long-term perspective on the part of a number of industrialized countries. Germany, Japan, and the United States are logical candidates to lead such an initiative.

However, the United States is in the least-favorable position to be able to help as it struggles with its own debt and trade problems. To assist in the environmental cleanup, the United States can contribute only $5 million each to Poland and Hungary, and participate with the EC to provide $5 million a year to an environmental center in Budapest. The U.S. Export-Import Bank (Eximbank) can extend no more than $600 million in direct loans throughout the world, with no funds specifically earmarked for U.S. business in Eastern Europe.

Japan, the world's largest capital exporter, is, clearly, in a better position to provide needed capital. The Japanese Eximbank has agreed to provide $500 million in loans to Poland and Hungary each. To help Poland support its currency, an additional loan of $150 million has been arranged. Japan also will provide technical assistance valued at $25 million to Poland and Hungary. Through 1987, commercial bank loans to six East European countries totaled over $9 billion.[15] The sum total of these initiatives exceeds the U.S. efforts by a considerable amount but is minuscule in comparison to the needs of the region. Further, the nonfinancial private sector has shown little enthusiasm for the Eastern section of Europe. Japanese manufacturers have preferred the United Kingdom, where they can build defenses against trade protectionism, and the Latin countries of Italy, Spain, and Portugal, where the governments are eager to construct the necessary infrastructures and/or labor is cheap.

Thus, among the three major economic powers, Germany has made the largest contribution to the East. Presently, reunification is the primary focus. Already, $200 billion was required to retire the worthless East Germany currency. Germany paid the Soviet Union an additional $12 billion to vacate. As many as 10,000 former officers of the East German military were retrained in 1990 at an average cost of over $11,000 each, another $119 million. Of course, these expenditures do not even begin to address the needs for housing, consumer goods, infrastructure, environmental cleanup, industrial modernization, and technology transfer.

Throughout Eastern Europe, worker morale is low, compounding the difficult situation. The economic pullout of the Soviet Union has sharply reduced output. In East Germany the collective agricultural system has nearly collapsed and unemployment lines are long. In neighboring Poland, unemployment could reach 11 percent, as industrial output declined 25 percent in 1990. Comparable declines in output were experienced in Hungary (10 percent), Romania (28 percent), and Bulgaria (30 percent).

The shift to more democratic systems of government and increased self-reliance have not resulted in an instantaneously higher standard of living. It appears that what the West Germans have almost miraculously achieved in just under 50 years, East Europeans expect to achieve in one to two years. Such high expectations can almost never be realized, certainly not in this case. East Germany is, perhaps, the most productive of the former Soviet satellites. Nevertheless, an East German worker is only 30 percent as productive as his West German counterpart. It will require many years and billions of dollars to change this situation.

Once again comparing the development of Asian NICs, worker expectations were substantially lower. Asian workers initially sought to acquire the basic necessities of adequate food and housing, with a modern refrigerator or television constituting their concept of luxury. The average East European is more likely to dream of trading his Trabant for a Mercedes.

The net effect of poor competitive position and unrealistic expectations is that the numbers of people immigrating from the East to the West are swelling and will continue to grow. And West Germany is the destination of choice. The working population of East Germany declined from 11 million in 1988 to 8.5 million in 1990. Up to 4 to 5 million Soviets of German descent could eventually find their way to the land of their ancestors. In Hungary, people wait in line to pay the equivalent of two weeks' salary for evening language classes, with most selecting English or German. It takes little imagination to guess the aspirations of those Hungarians who seek to learn the German language.

Thus, the pressure of immigration by East Europeans, the lack of a strong work ethic in those who do remain at home, and the billions of dollars required to rebuild the region will be problems that are left on the doorstep of West Germany. The West German desire to exploit the low-cost labor of Eastern Europe will backfire. The once-rich republic will find itself with more obligations than resources to fulfill them. Of course, the Germans will turn to their EC partners to help carry the load. However, given past hostilities and the more recent, economically motivated German superiority complex, the request for assistance will inspire little cooperation.

The inflation-phobic German government will be hesitant to print enough money to meet this challenge. Indeed, at such time as the ECU replaces national currencies, such an option would not be available. A more creative approach will be necessary. Countertrade may be a viable alternative.

COUNTERTRADE BETWEEN EASTERN EUROPE AND SUB-SAHARAN AFRICA

In the absence of strong trade links with the West, competitive labor force, and advanced technology, Eastern European countries will find it difficult to develop in the same manner as West Germany. They face two equally urgent needs: export markets for existing products and goods for domestic investment and consumption. Essentially, exports must be exchanged for goods needed for domestic use. However, because East European products may not compete successfully against American, Japanese, and German equivalents in Western markets, expansion in less-developed markets holds more promise.

Sub-Saharan Africa could be one of the best alternatives. The region is rich with raw materials and marketable commodities that have not been exploited primarily because of lack of capital investment. Mining industries that had been established during the colonial period of the Sub-Saharan were largely abandoned after independence in the 1960s. As a result, abundant natural resources remain untapped or underutilized, including iron ore, copper, zinc, nickel, gold, diamonds, and other industrial minerals.

As shown in Table 4.3, a number of Sub-Saharan countries with substantial mineral resources derive 50 percent or more of their export earnings from agricultural commodities. Only Zaire and Zambia earn the majority of export earnings from mineral-related industries. Thus, there is an opportunity for East European countries to trade either for raw materials to be used in industry or for gold and diamonds, which can be readily sold for hard currency.

In addition, this arrangement could encompass building materials for the construction of new industrial facilities and residential dwellings in Eastern Europe. The Ivory Coast, Ghana, Cameroon, Zaire,

TABLE 4.3
Selected Sub-Saharan Countries' Mineral Deposits and Primary Exports, 1984/1985

	Major Mineral Deposits	Product	Exports Amount(1)	%(2)
Cameroon	gold	coffee	$227	28.4%
		cocoa	176	21.9
		rough wood	79	9.8
		aluminum	67	8.4
Central African Republic	diamonds	coffee	31	35.4
	gold	rough wood	21	23.6
		cotton	13	14.5
Ghana	gold	cocoa	390	66.1
	diamonds	aluminum	33	5.7
Guinea-Bissau	iron ore	oil seeds, nuts	9	64.3
Kenya	gold	coffee	283	27.3
		tea	257	24.8
		petroleum products	176	16.7
Mozambique	gold	fresh fish	29	36.0
	coal	fresh fruit	16	19.4
Sudan	gold	cotton	237	47.7
		oil seeds, nuts	74	14.8
		live animals	70	14.1
Zaire	diamonds	copper	436	44.7
	copper	crude petroleum	218	22.3
	gold	coffee	186	19.0
	coal	diamonds	104	10.7
	copper			
Zambia	copper	copper	525	87.7
	coal	zinc	11	1.9
Zimbabwe	coal	tobacco	224	22.9
	gold	pig iron	118	12.1
		cotton	93	9.5

Notes: (1) millions of U.S. dollars; (2) percentage of total exports.
Source: Author's calculations based on United Nations. *Handbook of International Trade and Development Statistics, 1988.* New York: United Nations, 1988, pp. 192-213.

and Zimbabwe produce suitable, high-quality timber. In addition, Kenya has cement-producing capabilities.

Of course, East European countries lack adequate hard currency to purchase these materials in the conventional way. However, the variety of their manufactured exports is probably sufficient to negotiate a reasonable exchange of raw materials for manufactured goods. Sub-Saharan African countries are the most economically deprived in the world and have essentially been excluded from world trade activity. Accordingly, they face a desperate shortage of food and consumer goods, with most Sub-Saharan residents depending on subsistence farming for their livelihood.

At the same time, East European countries produce industrial and agricultural machines, fabricated metal (pipes and tubes), electronics, ships and boats, motor and railroad vehicles, clothing, and footwear. Exchanging these items for petroleum, clean coal, iron ore, timber, and cement would enable Eastern Europe to sustain needed reconstruction and improve current levels of industrial output. Both the construction and manufacturing activities would help resolve the region's current unemployment problems.

Of course, expanded African mining activities will require a certain amount of capital investment that neither the residents of the region nor East Europeans currently have any way of obtaining. Germany will need to provide start-up capital to facilitate this exchange mechanism.

However, it may not be a German who takes the initiative. The inspiration may come through Pope John Paul II, head of the Roman Catholic Church. The Polish Pope has both a personal friendship with Lech Walesa, former head of the labor union Solidarity and current political head of state, and a mission to enlarge the Catholic Church in Africa. Being keenly aware of the critical needs on both continents, the Pope may act as a catalyst to this process.

At first glance, countertrade could appear to be a roundabout way to spur East European development. Would it not be infinitely easier to simply attract foreign capital to Europe? The problem with such a direct approach is that it will take more time than the Europeans have. While waiting for the right joint ventures and needed technology transfers to materialize, the East European people will have few hard currency outlets for their products. This, in turn, means limited imports of raw materials and consumer goods. The result will be higher unemployment and deprivation. Even if Germany were able to miraculously transform the East to high-tech, low-cost producers overnight, where would the output be sold? There is some finite limit to the amount of export goods that current world markets can absorb.

On the other hand, East European/Sub-Saharan trade is not at all well developed. Table 4.4 shows that East European countries ship 6 percent or less of total exports to developing countries in Africa, while 36 percent to 72 percent goes to other East European countries. Since the old communist trading block is falling apart, this heavy reliance on socialist neighbors will not be sustainable. Soviet trade already has declined substantially. Further, most Easterners probably would prefer higher-quality Western goods.

TABLE 4.4
Highlighted Trade Patterns of Eastern Europe and Selected Countries in Sub-Saharan Africa

(in percentages)

Eastern Europe

Origin	Year	Destination	
		Eastern Europe	Developing Africa
Bulgaria	1980	66.6%	5.6%
Czechoslovakia	1986	72.0	2.5
Hungary	1987	50.1	2.7
Poland	1986	39.0	2.4
Romania	1985	36.2	5.8
USSR	1986	52.6	1.4
Yugoslavia	1987	34.2	5.7

Sub-Saharan Africa

Origin	Year	Destination	
		Eastern Europe	EC
Cameroon	1987	1.6%	68.3%
Central African Republic	1985	---	90.9
Ghana	1983	11.8	31.6
Guinea-Bissau	1981	---	62.0
Kenya	1984	0.5	45.2
Sudan	1983	8.6	25.2
Tanzania	1985	1.2	57.7
Zaire	1982	---	82.6
Zambia	1984	0.7	32.2

Note: The United Nations does not maintain trade statistics for the former East Germany.
Source: United Nations. *Handbook of International Trade and Development Statistics, 1988,* New York: United Nations, 1988, pp. 110–21.

Sub-Saharan exports to Eastern Europe (also shown in Table 4.4) are either nonexistent or relatively low. However, the EC represents a much more important export destination for those countries shown. The already-established trade ties between the two regions can facilitate both Germany's investment in the Sub-Saharan and the negotiation of countertrade arrangements with the East.

Thus, the expansion of production for trade in this fashion has several attractive features. It corrects underutilization in both developing regions. At the same time, the increased production would not have the effect of depressing world market prices since the additional supplies would be virtually equal to incremental demand. Most importantly, this is a viable solution to the critical development needs of both Eastern Europe and Sub-Saharan Africa.

JAPANESE EXPLOITATION OF GERMAN VULNERABILITY

The dynamics of European economic and political adjustments will not be lost on the Japanese. The Single European Market of 1992 represents relatively unexplored territory for Japanese conglomerates. While shipments to the United States (39 percent) and to Asia (23 percent) constituted 62 percent of total exports in 1987, only 17 percent of Japanese exports were destined for the EC. Part of the reason for this is that the EC has not allowed Japan the kind of free hand that it enjoys in the United States.

For example, the United States charges a 2.5 percent tariff on automobile imports. Individual states impose sales and gas-guzzler taxes, as applicable. In the EC, a value-added tax on all automobiles ranges from 14 percent in Germany to 500 percent in Greece. By January 1, 1993, value-added tax will be harmonized and a uniform import tariff of 10 percent will apply. In addition, specific countries have special rules for Japanese auto imports. In Italy, the limit is 3,000 units per year; in the United Kingdom, a 10 percent market share; and in France, a 3 percent market share. Thus, while the EC has held the line on Japanese auto imports, U.S. manufacturers have lost fully one-third of their domestic market.

Nevertheless, the Single European Market will make it easier for Japan to expand its market share of all goods, especially through direct investments in European subsidiaries. As recently as 1981, this region accounted for just under 9 percent of Japanese direct investment. By 1988, the share had doubled to 20 percent. Bank branches grew from two in 1987 to six in only one year. The prospect of only one bank license in order to operate throughout the EC would appear to be irresistible. In the same year, Japanese manufacturing subsidiaries grew from 300 to 400. The plan is, clearly, to become established in the EC, especially in the low-cost labor countries of Portugal, Spain, and Italy, distribute goods throughout the region after 1992, and avoid trade restrictions on imports.

Nissan, Toyota, and Mitsubishi already were producing commercial vehicles in Portugal by 1989. Nissan had also set up assembly operations in Spain, while its U.K. subsidiary maintained full manufacturing operations.

The automobile industry is certainly an area in which Japan and Germany will become even greater rivals. It is not the only area, however. Examining Table 4.5, one is struck by the number of industries in which Germany has earned significant shares of the world's export markets. Automobiles, nonelectric machines, organic and other chemicals, plastic materials, electric power machines, machines for special industries, and precision instruments are items for which German exports represent between 15 percent and 20 percent of world export market share. In total, the 15 categories in Table 4.5 accounted for over 53 percent of Germany's 1985 exports.

Comparing Japan's statistics to Germany's in the same 15 categories, one is also struck by the extent to which Japan already dominates Germany. For both countries, road motor vehicles are the primary export. Yet, while Germany exported vehicles worth $27 billion in 1985, the Japanese total was $39 billion. (The United States was a rather distant third at $18 billion.) In five other important German categories, the Japanese out-shipped the Germans by 70 percent or more. In two other areas, they were virtually tied. Thus, in eight of Germany's top 15 exports, Japan is already formidable competition.

In the same year, U.S. exports ($205 billion) exceeded those of both Germany ($183 billion) and Japan ($176 billion). However, the United States outperformed Germany and Japan in only five of the 15 categories that supplied over half of Germany's export earnings. Other categories that were among the top 15 for the United States included foodstuffs (corn, wheat, seeds, nuts, and kernels) and energy products (coal and petroleum products). Of course, these are products for which Germany has little competitive advantage and, therefore, will not be areas in which U.S. and German interests are in direct conflict.[16]

This view of German/Japanese competition is static and does not reveal the extent to which Japan has made inroads into the bread-and-butter of the export-driven German economy. Twelve of Germany's 15 top exports fall in the broad categories of (1) machinery and transport equipment and (2) chemicals. Table 4.6 shows what share of the export

TABLE 4.5
Export Mix and Market Share Comparisons — Germany, Japan, and the United States, 1985

Category	Germany		Japan		Exports U.S.	
	Amount	%	Amount	%	Amount	%
Road motor vehicles (732)	$27.1	18%	$39.0	26%	$18.3	12%
Nonelectric machines (719)	14.1	19	9.7	14	10.6	15
Organic chemicals (512)	6.5	18	2.4	7	5.2	14
Plastic materials (581)	6.0	20	(4)		3.6	12
Electrical machinery (729)	5.8	11	10.0	19	12.3	23
Electric power machines (722)	4.3	17	4.5	17	(5)	
Office machines (714)	4.1	9	7.7	16	14.3	30
Nonelectric power machines (711)	4.0	17	2.7	11	5.2	21
Machine for special industries (718)	4.0	12	3.8	12	8.5	26
Instruments, apparatus (861)	3.6	15	6.6	28	(5)	
Aircraft (734)	3.6	13	(4)		12.5	45
Chemicals – other (599)	3.2	19	(4)		(5)	
Telecommunications equipment (724)	2.7	8	11.7	33	3.8	11
Clothing not of fur (841)	2.6	7	(4)		(5)	
Iron & steel plate & sheet (674)	2.5	13	5.5	29	(5)	

Notes: Monetary amounts are billions of U.S. dollars; percentages are the country's share of world exports of the relevant item; numbers in parentheses are SITC (Standard International Trade Classification) codes; (4) = category is not among the top 16 Japanese exports; (5) = category is not among the top 16 U.S. exports.

Source: Author's calculations based on United Nations.' *Handbook of International Trade and Development Statistics, 1988.* New York: United Nations, 1988, pp. 192–213.

TABLE 4.6
World Export Shares — Germany, Japan, and the United States, 1970 and 1986

| | Machinery and Transport Equipment (7) | | | | Chemicals (5) | | | |
| | 1970 | | 1986 | | 1970 | | 1986 | |
	Amount	%	Amount	%	Amount	%	Amount	%
Total world exports	$89.8	100.0%	$721.1	100.0%	$22.1	100.0%	$178.2	100.0%
Export shares:								
Germany	$15.9	17.7%	$117.3	16.3%	$ 4.1	18.6%	$ 31.5	17.7%
Japan	7.8	8.7	133.3	18.5	1.2	5.4	9.4	5.3
United States	17.9	19.9	98.8	13.7	3.8	17.2	22.3	12.5
	$41.6	46.3%	$349.4	48.5%	$ 9.1	41.2%	$ 63.2	35.5%

Notes: Numbers in parentheses are SITC (Standard International Trade Classification) codes; monetary amounts are billions of U.S. dollars; and percentages are shares of world exports of the relevant item.
Source: Author's calculations based on United Nations. *Handbook of International Trade and Development Statistics, 1988.* New York: United Nations, 1988, pp. A24, A40, 136–57.

pie in these classifications was enjoyed by Germany, Japan, and the United States in 1970 and 1986.

In 1970, the United States held 20 percent of the machinery and transport equipment export market. Germany was a strong competitor with over 17 percent, while Japan enjoyed less than 9 percent. Sixteen years later, the U.S. share had plummeted to under 14 percent. Germany, too, had lost market share, but not nearly as much. Japan had surpassed both and commanded almost 19 percent of worldwide exports. Though the Japanese experience in the chemicals industry was not as dramatic, both Germany and the United States lost ground. Again, the United States was the biggest loser.

Lest one is tempted to believe that Germany was more successful in holding its market share because it was a better competitor, it is wise to recall that the United States has been a relatively easy market for any foreign company to enter and compete with. Historically, the diversity of national laws in Europe has made such activity more difficult. The Single European Market of 1992 should significantly reduce this difficulty. As it is, the 1987 share of Japanese exports to the EC (16.6 percent) was 37 percent higher than in 1970. The percentage of 1987 Japanese exports shipped to the United States (39.2 percent) had only grown by 15 percent from its 1970 base.

The trend is clear. Germany is likely to be the next economic superpower to feel the intense pressure of Japanese competition. It is not simply the attraction of a more open Europe that will bring the German/Japanese competition to a fever pitch. It is also the nature of the industries in which Germany is engaged.

To help clarify this point, Table 4.7 lists the 20 product classifications that generated the largest export revenues in 1985. Total shipments amounted to more than $1 trillion. All but two of Germany's top 15 exports are included among these top money makers. Thus, the conflict is inevitable. Germany represents an obstacle between Japan and its true domination of export markets worth more than $1 trillion a year.

Japanese exports already meet or exceed Germany's in 7 of the 20 categories.[17] In an eighth category (nonelectric machines), Japan is narrowing the gap. Two other categories (ships/boats at 32 percent and sound recorders/parts at 60 percent of world export share) are already under firm Japanese control. As a major contender in 10 of the top 20 markets, Japan probably will continue to push forward in those remaining markets that are feasible.

Three of these remaining markets are energy-related and, therefore, not promising from the Japanese perspective.[18] A fourth,

TABLE 4.7
Top 20 World Exports, 1985
(in millions of U.S. dollars)

Rank	SITC CODE	DESCRIPTION	TOTAL VALUE
1	331	Crude petroleum	$ 205,260
2	732	Road motor vehicles	148,890
3	332	Petroleum products	91,233
4	719	Nonelectric machines	71,053
5	729	Electric machinery - other	52,634
6	714	Office machines	46,930
7	841	Clothing, not of fur	39,927
8	341	Gas, natural & manufactured	38,537
9	512	Organic chemicals	36,156
10	724	Telecommunications equipment	35,260
11	711	Nonelectric power machinery	32,657
12	931	Special transactions	29,751
13	581	Plastic materials	29,303
14	734	Aircraft	27,585
15	722	Electric power machinery	25,540
16	718	Machinery for special industries	24,048
17	861	Instruments, apparatus	23,692
18	641	Paper and paperboard	22,086
19	735	Ships and boats	20,460
20	891	Sound recorders and parts	19,035
			$2,020,037

Note: SITC is an acronym for Standard International Trade Classification.
Source: Author's calculations based on United Nations. *Handbook of International Trade and Development Statistics, 1988*. New York: United Nations, 1988, pp. 180.

paper and paperboard, is too dependent on large timber resources to be a reasonable target for this wood-importing country. However, five of the remaining product classifications show more promise.[19]

All five of these should be considered prime candidates for fierce Japanese/German competition, as they are also currently among Germany's top 15 exports. In fact, as Germany finds itself preoccupied with the problems of reunification and eastward expansion throughout Europe, Japanese companies may exploit the situation.

As Germans are forced to make hard choices about cleaning up the environment and infrastructure of Eastern Europe versus opening more productive facilities to capture the low-cost labor available there, German capital availability certainly will be strained. The Japanese may come to the rescue with needed infusions, not for the environment, but to buy into those German companies engaged in the industries that are important to Japan and plan to set up production plants in Eastern Europe. In this way, Japanese partners will capture existing market shares and assure themselves of long-term low-cost labor pools, while the West Germans smooth over any troublesome cultural transitions.

GERMAN RETALIATION

German business will not necessarily sit still and permit the Japanese to proceed unchallenged with this agenda. Should the Germans decide to fight back, the automobile industry could become a primary arena for the conflict. Road motor vehicle exports are important to both countries, but are more important to Japan. While vehicle shipments were over 22 percent of Japan's total exports in 1985, they represented 15 percent in Germany.

Japanese car makers recently have begun to focus on the luxury segment of the auto industry. Honda introduced its Acura Legend in 1986. Three years later, Nissan's Infiniti and Toyota's Lexus emerged. Mazda and Mitsubishi are expected to follow suit in the near future. While these cars compete with U.S. luxury models, European upscale autos also have been targeted. In particular, the Lexus is frequently compared to the German-made Mercedes.

Toyota appears to take great pride in noting that the two cars receive comparable industry ratings, but that Lexus sells for $16,000 to $35,000 less than Mercedes. Such pride apparently is justified since the new Japanese entrant outsold both Mercedes and BMW in the U.S. market during the first nine months of 1990.

One suspects that the reason for this success is, indeed, the price differential. However, if Germany's luxury car makers designed lower-priced models of comparable quality, the consumer market probably would prefer the European versions. After all, for a prospective luxury car buyer, the choice between a Toyota and a Mercedes, at the same price, should represent a fairly easy decision.

Designing such models may not be as difficult as it sounds. There are a number of overseas locations with relatively low labor costs that German auto makers have not fully exploited. For an initiative aimed specifically at Japan, the most interesting locations are in Asia.

Indonesia is already host to eight Japanese assembly plants and four German — Volkswagen, Mercedes, BMW, and Opel. Once established, a full manufacturing facility could realize even more cost efficiencies. China has offered tax relief and other incentives for automobile-manufacturing joint ventures that export 70 percent of their production. Thus far, Volkswagen is the only German company to take advantage of this offer. Four Japanese firms have done so.

Taiwan and Thailand are particularly interested in becoming sites of home-grown motor vehicles. Taiwan offers tax inducements to foreign investors utilizing local design capabilities. To further increase Taiwanese involvement in the auto industry, all vehicles for local use must have at least 50 percent local content of materials and equipment. Given the wealth of Taiwan and the extent of its recent industrial advancement, a German/Taiwanese joint venture may be quite feasible.

Thailand already has used its 45 percent local content law to bring itself to the point of nearly being capable of producing vehicles for export. In addition to seven Japanese companies in Thailand, Volkswagen and BMW have production facilities.

In a sense, it would be poetic justice if, while Japanese car makers rush to set up plants in Europe to evade import restrictions and to prepare for the Single European Market, their German counterparts take the same approach in Asia. Such an arrangement probably would be more a shock to the Japanese than to the Germans. German auto manufacturers have successfully competed with Rolls Royce, Rover, Jaguar, Peugeot, Ferrari, Maserati, and others within the EC. Japanese auto makers have never had any meaningful competition on Asian soil.

Of course, this approach could work equally well in other industries. China, South Korea, Taiwan, and others are all eager to import technology in order to increase the value-added content of industrial output. In other words, these countries recognize the need to replace relatively simple assembly operations with production that requires more advanced skills. Up to this point, it has been primarily Japan that facilitated this process. However, that could change if Germany decides to defend itself more aggressively against a Japanese economic assault.

BEFORE THE DUST SETTLES

As appealing as the analogy between the United States and the European Community may be, the transition to a unified Europe will not be easy. National interests will always be more compelling than the European agenda. Egocentric power struggles among heads of state will not cease. The situation will only be complicated by the political and economic realignment of Eastern Europe. In the process of such widespread change and restructuring, Germany, heir apparent to the role of head European economic power, will be caught up in addressing the nearly unrealizable demands of Eastern Europe and in fighting off Japanese competition.

Meanwhile, the United Kingdom should be spared most of this agony, since its government elected to discipline itself and the rest of the country during the 1980s. The resulting strength of the United Kingdom may be one of the most surprising developments after 1992. Nevertheless, this exercise in regionalization should prove to be one of the most interesting chapters in the world's economic history.

NOTES

1. The 12 member countries are Belgium, France, Italy, Luxembourg, the Netherlands, the new reunified Germany, Denmark, Ireland, the United Kingdom, Greece, Portugal, and Spain.

2. The original members were Belgium, France, Italy, Luxembourg, the Netherlands, and West Germany. Denmark, Ireland, and the United Kingdom joined in 1973. During the 1980s, new members included Greece (1981), Portugal (1985), and Spain (1985).

3. The EEC merged with the European Coal and Steel Community and the European Atomic Energy Community.

4. The concept of exchange rate parities had been initiated with the 1944 Bretton Woods agreement among members of the International Monetary Fund. Most exchange rates were effectively tied to the U.S. dollar. The Bretton Woods arrangement broke down in the early 1970s, freeing most currencies to float. The Werner Report recommended that the EC members continue to tie their exchange rates within the EC.

5. Currently, individual check and credit card transactions also may be denominated in ECUs.

6. The EC Commission makes policy proposals. The EC Council is the Community's decision-making body; there are, in addition, specialist councils. The 518-member EC Parliament usually has the right to render an opinion on a specific proposal.

7. NATO is the North Atlantic Treaty Organization, a military alliance between Belgium, Canada, Denmark, France, Great Britain, Iceland, Italy, Luxembourg, the Netherlands, Norway, Portugal, the United States, Greece, Turkey, and Germany.

8. Exports and imports in the United Kingdom in 1983 and 1988 were as follows (in billions) (*International Financial Statistics*, May 1990):

	1983		1988	
	$US	£	$US	£
Exports	92.0	80.4	143.5	107.6
Imports	93.6	77.9	180.5	125.2

9.   Indeed, banks in the United Kingdom held more foreign deposits than those in any other country. Japan and the United States followed with $845.7 billion and $667.7 billion, respectively (*International Financial Statistics*, May 1990).

10.   The Asian NICs are Hong Kong, Singapore, South Korea, and Taiwan.

11.   Poland ($40 billion) and Hungary ($18 billion) accounted for the majority of East European external debt in 1989.

12.   The developing countries of Europe and the Mediterranean include Cyprus, Greece, Hungary, Malta, Poland, Portugal, Romania, Turkey, and Yugoslavia.

13.   Developing countries of East Asia and the Pacific include China, Indonesia, South Korea, Laos, Malaysia, Papua New Guinea, the Philippines, Solomon Islands, Thailand, Tonga, Vanuatu, and Western Samoa.

14.   In 1988, debt to GNP in Europe was 44 percent, while in 1980, the Asian ratio was 17 percent.

15.   Loans to the six countries were distributed as follows (in billions of dollars) (Horisaka, 1989):

East Germany	2.9
Poland	0.7
Hungary	3.3
Bulgaria	1.1
Czechoslovakia	0.6
Yugoslavia	0.8

16.   Instead, agricultural confrontations are more likely to involve the United States seeking freer access to the European agricultural market. These agricultural shipments will not directly threaten German economic activity.

17.   The seven categories are road motor vehicles, other electrical machinery, office machines, telecommunications equipment, nonelectric power machinery, electric power machinery, and instruments and apparatus.

18.   These three are crude petroleum, petroleum products, and natural and manufactured gas.

19.   These include organic chemicals, plastic materials, machines for special industries, aircraft, and clothing not of fur.

5

Integration of the Soviet Union and Eastern Europe into World Economic Markets: A Difficult Process

THE FUTURE: A FUNCTION OF THE PAST

After more than 40 years of virtual isolation from Western markets, the Soviet Union and Eastern Europe seek to participate in the capitalist experience, that is, to become part of the global economy. The countries seek foreign investment capital and, until their crippled markets can be reconstructed, foreign aid. The irony is, of course, that these same countries have spent decades constructing ideological, military, and trade barriers between the East and the West. Such barriers do not evaporate overnight.

To complicate matters, the Soviet Union appears determined to abide by terms of conditionality that allow it to have its cake and eat it, too. Instead of admitting that its mismanagement has devastated the region and that it has the responsibility to fully utilize its own assets to atone for past abuse and to alleviate current deprivation, the Soviet Union appears intent on walking away from Eastern Europe and solving its own redundant labor problem by allowing the survival of the fittest to drive work force adjustments. Perhaps, foreigners will step in and ease the strain. After all, the Soviet Union appears willing to a-gree to not start a nuclear or large-scale conventional war. In the Soviet way of thinking, that should be sufficient to stimulate Western concern for Eastern Europe and the USSR, particularly in the United States.

However, the actual transition from communist to capitalist will not be a short, straight line. Holding onto the sacredness of central planning, the Soviet Union, Romania, and Bulgaria probably will find the road to economic prosperity long and rocky. At the same time,

Yugoslavia, Hungary, and Czechoslovakia may have the option of becoming part of the European Community (EC) and potentially facing economic domination by Germany. However, this prospect may hold limited appeal. Yugoslavia chose neutrality as early as 1948. Hungary and Czechoslovakia may find EC/German domination no more enticing than Soviet control. A neutral trading block of these three countries could prove to be a more palatable and effective mechanism.

Poland also could be brought into this alliance. A neutral Poland would relieve Germany of the need to absorb the economic problems of its eastern neighbor. Since there is no love lost between the Germans and the Poles, such an arrangement would meet with little opposition in either country. Further, a neutral Poland might constitute an effective buffer between Germany and the Soviet Union, making it possible for Germany to renegotiate the bilateral agreements reached at the time of German reunification.

THE SHREWD SOVIET DEAL WITH THE GERMANS

In all fairness, there is substantial incentive for Germany to seek to relieve itself of obligations to the Soviet Union. The ruin of Eastern Germany may be directly attributed to Soviet mismanagement and/or influence via Erich Honeker.[1] As a result, western Germany, second only to the United States in export strength and renowned for high-quality output, finds itself wed to a country with an industrial infrastructure (built before 1920) that produces goods for which there are virtually no buyers. To have to pay for the privilege of assuming this monstrous responsibility appears to be, at best, counterintuitive.

In fact, one wonders why the Germans negotiated such an arrangement in the first place. One possible explanation is that political implications carried more weight than economic considerations. A clear winner has been German Chancellor Helmut Kohl. His political star never rose higher than at the time of the October 1990 reunification.

Shortly thereafter, Kohl easily won the election for chancellor of the united Germany. His campaign pledge was that Western investors would rush into eastern Germany with abundant capital for restructuring and, therefore, that no tax increases would be necessary. His challenger, Oskar LaFontaine, delivered a distinctly different message. He suggested that industrial and social infrastructure repair would be a prerequisite to attracting foreign investment. This would take both time and money. Living conditions in the East would not improve right away and tax increases would be inevitable.

The German populace clearly preferred Kohl's less ominous assessment of the situation. However, the tab for East German industrial modernization, infrastructure repair and construction, and environmental cleanup has been estimated at roughly DM1 trillion, or $600 billion. This is not an insignificant sum, even for Germany.

West German merchandise trade surpluses during the ten years ended 1989 totaled only $404 billion, $196 billion less than the needed $600 billion. During the same ten years, the net amount of foreign direct investment by Germans, the sort of outlays that will be necessary in the East, amounted to only $52 billion. While annual government revenues are typically in the $350 billion range, expenditures have exceeded revenues in every year since 1974. The resulting fiscal deficits have not been troublesome for the country because of the strength of the private sector. However, it appears that the private sector may be placed under considerable strain to effect the East German reconstruction.

Of course, the Soviet Union is not being held accountable for any portion of these costs. Quite the contrary, the economic and social provisions of the treaty between Bonn and East Berlin specify that the contractual obligations between the German Democratic Republic and the Soviet Union will be honored. These contractual obligations will result in substantial East Germany trade surpluses with the Soviet Union, that is, Germany shipping more goods to the USSR than it receives. The Bonn government also announced in 1990 that it would cover a major part of the cost of retraining and housing for Soviet military personnel returning to the USSR, as well as upkeep for the forces that will remain in eastern Germany.

Even before reunification, a consortium of German banks agreed to provide the Soviets an almost $2 billion line of credit to help finance the modernization of food and consumer-goods industries. The Bonn government also agreed (in 1990) to guarantee bank loans of DM5 billion to the USSR at below-market rates and without project specificity. It is anticipated that more economic assistance programs will follow. Simply stated, Germany is rewarding the Soviet Union for abusing the eastern portion of the unified country. All that is being asked in return is that the Soviets leave quietly.

Two outcomes of this arrangement appear likely. As the realities of reunification become clearer, the German people will begin to understand the burden that Kohl placed on their shoulders while insisting that the whole exercise would be effortless. From a historical perspective, Helmut Kohl may become to Germany what Roger Smith is to General Motors, a leader who transformed an apparently smooth-running, world-class organization into an unwieldy bureaucracy struggling to remain competitive, but weighed down by the results of ill-advised, short-sighted decisions in the past. History will not be kind to Chancellor Kohl. The second outcome follows the first and may be even more immediate. If the deals struck between the German and Soviet governments placed unfair burdens on the German people, such contracts will lose their legitimacy. Any reasonable opportunity to nullify the agreements probably will be seized.

THE RICHES OF THE SOVIET UNION

Even if Germany does withdraw economic support, the USSR will hardly be without resources. The Soviet Union is one of the richest countries in the world in terms of natural resources.

More crude oil is produced in the USSR than in any other single country. In 1986, this production totalled 615 million metric tons (or 4.474 billion barrels).[2] Table 5.1 shows that the Soviet Union produces almost as much oil as the second and third largest producers (the United States and Saudi Arabia) combined. In fact, Soviet production is large by any number of comparisons. It is greater than the combined output of the United States and the United Kingdom (549.4 mmt).

TABLE 5.1
Crude Oil Production, 1986
(in million metric tons)

Country	Units of Production
Soviet Union	615.0
United States	428.2
Saudi Arabia	251.7
China	130.6
Mexico	126.2
United Kingdom	121.2
Venezuela	94.0
Iran	93.4
Iraq	82.7
Nigeria	72.8
Kuwait	71.5
United Arab Emirates	66.2
	2,153.5
World	2,800.0

Source: U.S. Department of Commerce, Bureau of the Census. *Statistical Abstract of the United States, 1989*, 109e. Washington, D.C.: U.S. Department of Commerce, 1989, p. 833.

China, Mexico, Venezuela, and Nigeria together pumped less than 70 percent of 1986 Soviet oil production (423.6 mmt). Perhaps the most graphic comparison is that not even Saudi Arabia, Iran, Iraq, Kuwait, and the United Arab Emirates produced more oil (565.5 mmt) than the USSR.[3]

Soviet activity amounts to approximately 22 percent of world output. At 1986 prices, the market value of this production was $61.8 billion.[4] At the 1990 price of $25 per barrel, the value is closer to $112 billion. Since the USSR exports approximately 16 percent of its crude oil to the West in exchange for hard currency, this translates into hard-currency earnings of $10 to $18 billion. It should be noted that Soviet crude oil exports to socialist countries in Eastern Europe and to other developing countries are more than 2-1/2 times those to the developed West.

Natural gas production, an extension of crude oil exploration, is becoming increasingly important as a hard-currency earner. In 1986, natural gas exports brought in 28 percent of the amount of crude oil sales to the West.

Coal is another abundant natural resource in the USSR. Table 5.2 shows that the Soviet Union produced 16 percent of world coal production in 1986, ranking third behind China and the United States. At 1986 prices, this output was worth $20 billion.[5]

This abundant endowment is not limited to fossil fuels. In 1986, the Soviet Union ranked first in the production of iron ore, lead, manganese

TABLE 5.2
Coal Production, 1986

(in million metric tons)

Country	Units of Production
China	840.0
United States	738.9
Soviet Union	512.9
Poland	192.1
South Africa	175.7
India	166.1
Australia	133.4
United Kingdom	108.1
	2,867.2
World	3,195.0

Source: U.S. Department of Commerce, Bureau of the Census. *Statistical Abstract of the United States, 1989,* 109e. Washington, D.C.: U.S. Department of Commerce, 1989, p. 833.

ore, nickel, nitrogen (in ammonia), and marketable potash and held second place in gold and platinum (after South Africa), chromite (again, after South Africa), zinc (after Canada), cement (after China), and aluminum, sulfur, and phosphate (all after the United States). While not among the top three producers of diamonds, the USSR also has sizeable diamond fields.

With so much wealth virtually lying in the ground, it is difficult to understand why the economy should be in such disarray. Why are store shelves empty? Why do Soviets fear starvation? It is certainly not because there is no food production. The 1986 Soviet wheat crop was 62 percent larger than its U.S. counterpart and slightly larger than Chinese output.[6] In the same year, Soviet commercial fishermen reeled in nearly as much as the Japanese, 40 percent more than the Chinese, and more than twice as much as the Americans.[7] One would not expect meat to be in short supply, either, since the 1986 volume of meat prepared for consumption in the Soviet Union constituted 74 percent and 81 percent of Chinese and U.S. production, respectively.[8]

Admittedly, the Soviet Union has a larger population, in other words, more mouths to feed, than Japan and the United States. It is also true that Japan is a net importer of food. As Table 5.3 shows, in 1987 Japan imported $23 billion more in food items than it exported. The Japanese land mass is less than 2 percent of that of the Soviet, while the Japanese population is 43 percent of the Soviet.[9] The level of Japanese food importation becomes reasonable in light of these comparisons.

TABLE 5.3
Food Exports and Imports — Soviet Union, Japan, United States, and China

		Food Trade (1)		
Year	Country	Exports	Imports	Balance
1986	Soviet Union	$ 1,538	$16,219	$(14,681)
1987	Japan	1,626	24,288	(22,662)
1987	United States	28,332	27,372	960
1985	China	4,561	1,874	2,687

Note: (1) millions of dollars.
Source: U.S. Department of Commerce, Bureau of the Census. *Statistical Abstract of the United States, 1989*, 109e. Washington, D.C.: U.S. Department of Commerce, 1989, p. 833.

However, in roughly the same period, the Soviet Union was a net importer of food valued at $15 billion. Even when the barren wasteland of Siberia is excluded from the USSR land mass, the area of Japan still represents less than 3 percent.[10] That the two countries should have such similar net food import bills is difficult to reconcile.

The population of the United States is 86 percent of that of the Soviet Union, while its area is two-thirds that of the more fully inhabited (non-Siberian) Soviet Union. Nevertheless, the United States is a net food exporter. This is true despite the fact that the United States grows less wheat and realizes a lower yield from commercial fishing than the USSR.

With approximately the same area of the United States, China feeds a population that is almost four times that of the Soviet. Even though China produces less wheat, catches less fish, and produces not much more meat than the Soviet Union, China was a net exporter of food in 1985.

Such differences may not be attributed solely to distribution inequities. The number of nonmarine commercial vehicles of all kinds in the Soviet Union is almost six times as large as the Chinese equivalent. Further, the Soviet merchant fleet has in excess of 50 percent more capacity.[11]

In the face of these endowments of overabundant natural resources, competitive agricultural capabilities, and apparently adequate distribution facilities, the often-described desperation of the Soviet people does not ring true. How can a country with so much have so little?

DECADES OF SOVIET MISMANAGEMENT

The most plausible explanation for these contradictions is that the people and resources of the Soviet Union have been grossly mismanaged since the October Revolution in 1917. In the process, natural resource endowments, the quest for individual excellence, and the natural catalyst of economically stimulated competition became worthless. Essentially, all activities were geared so that a uniform level of mediocrity could be achieved.

In this sense, the goal of the central government has been realized beyond its wildest collective imagination. Left to his own devices, the average Soviet would not know where to begin if asked to make an economically sound business decision.

This disregard for the value of resources, and even human life, enables Soviet officials to turn to the West and ask for assistance — indeed, for a bailout. Essentially, they place no more value on Western resources than they do their own. Why should they have to grapple with the problem of getting their own food to their own people when someone else can do it for them? Besides, if enough Soviets go hungry for long enough, there will be fewer to complain and to disturb the natural order.

These assertions may appear overly harsh at first glance. However, upon closer examination, these conclusions appear to be well supported. The basic tenet of Marxism is that capitalism results in inequities of income, wealth, and power. While this assumption is not altogether untrue, the appropriate actions prescribed by Marxism do little to correct this.

Under the Soviet version of government, all productive and financial resources belonged to the state. An individual earned his livelihood through working for wages. Wages were set by the government and there were few incentives for performing above the government-specified norm or quota. With the state guarantee of employment, there also were few penalties for operating below norm.

In the event that the country recognized some economic windfall due to exogenous factors, individuals realized no appreciable change in their standard of living. Instead, the unexpected wealth was added to government coffers. It was then up to the government to decide whether the proceeds should be distributed to the people.

In the 1970s, the Soviet Union benefitted from the increases in oil prices, as did all other oil-exporting countries. The total value of exported fuel went from $2 billion in 1970 to $10.4 billion in 1975 to $35.9 billion in 1980. The implied average annual growth rate from 1970 to 1975 is 39 percent. During the second half of the decade, the value of fuel exports increased 28 percent a year. Even with the high inflation rates of the 1970s, real increases in revenues were substantial. Yet the Soviet growth rate of real per capita income fell from 4.9 percent in the first half of the 1970s to 3.3 percent in the second half. The average increase from 1980 to 1987 was an even lower 2.5 percent.

The coincidence of oil revenue increases and slower growth in per capita income is hardly accidental. The Soviet central process would probably not have achieved a worse economic outcome if its stated objective was failure. Large investment projects were planned and financed by the central government. Actual implementation was the responsibility of specific enterprises via government ministries. Yet the local ministries and enterprise were not accountable for any outcome. They were not required to repay the monies or to generate a profit.

They were not even pressed to finish the project, because evaluations were based on the amount of work in progress. Thus, the magnitude of uncompleted projects was more important than the extent to which projects came to fruition. In the 1960s, the average time required to complete a major Soviet project was 7 to 8 years, 250 percent of the time that was necessary to complete a project in the West. By the 1970s, this average had grown to 8 to 10 years.

The decision with respect to a particular proposed project was negotiated among the central government, the appropriate ministry, and the specific enterprise that would implement the project. Proposed projects were almost always of the expansion variety, because innovation and improvement of existing operations were not rewarded. In the quest for mediocrity, it was far more rational to expand production of obsolete goods using out-of-date technology than to design a more competitive product or methodology.

The result was predictable. Valuable resource inputs were wasted to produce inferior end products. The opportunity cost of a wasteful production approach was never analyzed. The Soviets even imported low-tech Western investment goods and failed to utilize them, leaving many neither installed nor used.

In terms of accountability, an enterprise was rewarded for quantity, not quality. Thus, other enterprises worked with the inferior output of this process. For example, an enterprise must typically work with a computer that has been constructed using 20-year-old technology. This is true despite the fact that fourth- or fifth-generation machines are produced in the Soviet Union. Only the top leaders of the country, the elite, have access to the more modern versions.

Of course, this condition is not limited to business enterprises. The quality of many consumer goods is so low that Soviet households refuse to buy them. In 1983, the central government estimated that 500,000 television sets, 115,000 radios, 250,000 cameras, 1.5 million watches, and 160,000 refrigerators sat, unsalable, in Soviet warehouses.

Not only was there no attention to quality within industrial enterprises, but once projects were planned and initiated, no social infrastructure was included in the plans. Schools, medical facilities, retail establishments, and apartments were essentially ignored. In the late 1980s, less than 74 percent of Soviet residences had hot running water. Outside urban areas, 15 percent lacked bathroom facilities. Of the approximately 4,000 rural hospitals, 2,600 (65 percent) had no hot water and 1,080 (27 percent) operated without sewage facilities.

Because of the poor condition of the Soviet infrastructure and agricultural industry, a large percentage of the annual grain harvest never gets to market. It either rots before it can be harvested or is spilled while being transported over rough terrain. Of the total 1988 grain harvest of 210 million metric tons, 20 million tons rotted before harvesting and 15 million tons spilled on the way to market.

It seems inconceivable that a major producer of cement, iron ore, and aluminum could not construct a better supply of agricultural machinery or a more adequate roadway system. Soviet roads cover only about the same distance as those in Belgium, a country only slightly larger than the state of Maryland.

Food transport is also heavily dependent on the country's rail system. Yet only half of the perishables shipped by rail can be transported in refrigerated cars. To suggest that a country that exports over $9 billion in sophisticated weapons to the nonsocialist Third World cannot construct a functional rail system for food transportation is ludicrous.

A more reasonable explanation is that the military psyche of the government predisposes the country to a backward transportation system. More advanced road and rail networks might make it too easy for enemy troops to invade. The tragic loss of 20 million Soviet lives during World War II appears to have been the justification for many of the decisions of the central government. The Soviet defense budget has consistently represented from 12 percent to 17 percent of gross national product. In the United States, the percentage is closer to 6 percent. American armed forces number roughly 2.3 million personnel, while Soviet armed forces include 4.4 million people.

The Soviet priorities are clearly skewed toward military pursuits. During the 1970s, the USSR developed or substantially improved 11 nuclear missile systems: six intercontinental and five submarine-launched ballistic missiles. As a point of comparison, the United States developed one intercontinental and two submarine-launched systems. More to the point, the Soviets realized large oil-related revenue increases in the 1970s and did not use them to improve the living standards or industrial competitiveness of the country. They were used instead to finance an all-out arms race with the United States.

Now that the decades of neglect have produced insufferable conditions that the central government can no longer ignore, the Soviets are asking that the West forgive and forget and treat the USSR as any other struggling, less-developed nation. The Soviet mandate to the West appears to be clear:

1. give financial and technical aid,
2. do not expect the Soviet Union to relinquish its assets,
3. do not expect the Soviet Union to adjust its foreign trade with respect to arms shipments or artificially high import prices of

goods received from politically important trading partners, such as Cuba and Nicaragua,

4. do not hold the USSR accountable for past misdeeds, and
5. assume full responsibility for now economically devastated Eastern Europe.

One senses little commitment on the part of the Soviet government either to actively participate in the real reforms that will be necessary domestically or to assist Eastern Europe in its reconstruction.

THE STRAINED EVOLUTION OF EASTERN EUROPE

Eastern Europe will not be integrated into the mainstream of the industrialized West as rapidly as many of its residents anticipate. Even before the October Revolution in 1917, Eastern Europe was plagued with economic backwardness that was not noted in Western Europe. While scientific inquiry and philosophical development flourished in the West, eastern states struggled under first one and then another system of landlords that discouraged entrepreneurship and commercial growth.

Poland lost its independence in 1697 to Saxony (Germany), shortly before the Industrial Revolution began in Britain in 1750. The arts and sciences that had enjoyed significant development for approximately 200 years beginning in the late fourteenth century lost momentum as Sweden and Russia claimed Polish land. Saxon rule followed. In the late eighteenth century, the country was divided among Prussia (Germany), Austria, and Russia and disappeared from the map of Europe. Upon reunification and independence after World War I, its republican constitution was quickly replaced by dictatorship and then military rule. Shortly after World War II, the Communist Party gained control.

Bulgaria and Romania were ruled by the Turkish Ottoman Empire from the thirteenth and fourteenth centuries, respectively. Both remained essentially agricultural states even after their independence.[12] The early years of Bulgarian independence were overseen first by a czar and then by a dictator. The Communists took over in 1944 and began the first moves toward industrialization. Thus, Bulgaria has known only the communist form of industry throughout its history.

Romania's independence from the Ottoman Empire was followed by a similar sequence of governments, with the additional problems of violence and corruption. Again, upon communist takeover, Romanian industrial development began. However, in the early 1960s, the Romanian government initiated a policy of separation from the Soviet Union but did not liberalize the business environment. Quite the contrary, every phase of production and consumption remained under the strict control of central government.

Hungary and most of Yugoslavia also were held by the Turks until the eighteenth and nineteenth centuries. Parts of Yugoslavia (Montenegro in 1799 and Serbia in 1829) gained independence relatively early. However, the Croatian region of the country went from domination by Turks to domination by Austrians (Hapsburg Empire).[13] The Slovenian region of Yugoslavia had been in Austrian hands since 1335. Early in the eighteenth century, the Hapsburgs also took Hungary from the Turks.

The three Czechoslovakian regions of Bohemia, Moravia, and Slovakia were also part of the Austrian Empire as early as 1526. All the Austrian territories continued to be held when the Hapsburg Empire was reorganized as the Austro-Hungarian Monarchy. Austrian rule ceased when the monarchy was dissolved at the end of World War I.

Thus, Eastern Europe is the product of a progression of invasion, occupation, and colonization. Romania was the first to gain independence in 1878. By that time, Britain, France, Germany, and the United States were all well on their way to becoming strong industrial powers. Romania had not even begun. As other countries in the region gained independence, they were even further behind. To the extent that political turmoil distracted from economic development, Eastern Europe continued to stagnate.

Even though the end of World War I brought liberation to Poland, Czechoslovakia, Hungary, and parts of Yugoslavia, prosperity did not follow. The introduction of Communism after World War II would presumably bring these countries into the modern age of industry. The cruel irony is that the Soviet influence in this region not only did not deliver a higher standard of living to people that had already been victimized, but it also installed systems of government and industry that have limited their ability to understand and effect needed change. At precisely the moment of greatest need in Eastern Europe, the Soviet Union has "liberated" its former satellites.

A NEUTRAL TRADING BLOCK

The economically devastated countries of the region may find the difficult process of development somewhat easier if they band together to coordinate their strengths and collectively compensate for their weaknesses. During the interwar period, most of their external trade had been with other countries in Europe. It was only after Moscow's 1949 creation of the Council for Mutual Economic Assistance (CMEA) that East European shipments became destined primarily for the Soviet Union. CMEA was engineered to retaliate against the Marshall Plan, a kind of economic turf battle. The problem with the CMEA was that the economic assistance, in the final analysis, was not mutual.

Because of the noncompetitive nature of most East European industry and monetary systems, EC membership is not currently feasible. The countries that would most benefit from such a nonaligned trading block are Czechoslovakia, Hungary, and Yugoslavia.

Czechoslovakia already possesses a relatively well-disciplined work force and has announced its intentions to follow the model of a West European country in terms of market-oriented systems. Along these lines, Czechoslovakia reduced its financing facilities for exports of equipment and arms in 1987. Since Czech shipments to the developed world are composed primarily of fuels and raw materials, the 1987 decision served to reduce exports to developing countries. Already, Czechoslovakia holds claims on developing nations (primarily from trade credits) of $2 to $3 billion. Reducing the uncompensated outflow of goods to such trading partners will make sorely needed domestic investment and convertible currency exports somewhat easier.

From an exchange rate of 5.35 korunas to the dollar in 1988, the Czechoslovakian government devalued the currency to 14.3 korunas in 1989 for all trade with nonsocialist countries and further to 17.0 korunas in 1990. Clearly, these actions are intended to encourage nonsocialist trade. At the same time, the value of the currency has been increased relative to the ruble in order to discourage trade with the Soviet Union.

Hungary also has introduced measures to curtail shipments to nonconvertible currency nations. Further, the forint, Hungary's monetary unit, is tied to a basket of convertible currencies. Domestically, price reform removed many consumer items from government control. In 1988, the percentage of consumer goods with free-market prices increased to 53 percent. By early 1990, it was up to 77 percent.

The tax system, which had been differentiated in its treatment of state enterprises, cooperatives, nonsocialist enterprises, and joint ventures, was modified in 1989 to a single, unified code. This creates a level playing field for all businesses. Even more significantly, commercial banking has been liberalized. Beginning in 1987, the National Bank of Hungary became a central bank more like the U.S.

Federal Reserve and a total of five competitive commercial banks was established.

The most advanced financial system of Eastern Europe, indeed, of socialist countries, is in Yugoslavia. Since 1971, the government has used the banking system to effect macroeconomic adjustments. Also, commercial banks, investment banks, and other financial institutions are currently in operation. Significantly, investment decisions rest with the investor. However, 80 percent to 90 percent of Gross State Product is concentrated in large-scale operations in the social sector and financial discipline has left much to be desired. Even substantial operating losses have been readily financed in this "easy-money" environment. This situation led to consumer inflation rates of 200 percent and 1,200 percent in 1988 and 1989, respectively.

These three countries, to a greater or lesser extent, are all struggling with the challenges of reform. However, each has made significant progress in at least one aspect of increased free-market orientation. Czechoslovakia has legislated substantial changes in the guidelines for industrial formation and operation. Hungary has concentrated more on financial reform. Yugoslavia enjoys relatively greater access to Western markets.[14]

However, no synergies can be realized from the competitive advantages as long as the countries fail to cooperate with each other. It should be remembered that, as part of the Austro-Hungarian Monarchy, each contributed to its success, albeit involuntarily. Further, since each has a comparable population base and economic standing, one has little to fear from the others.[15]

EXPLOITING THEIR COMPETITIVE ADVANTAGES

Czechoslovakia is the most attractive country in terms of foreign direct investment in industry. More specifically, the Bohemian and Moravian regions hold the greatest promise, with Bohemia being the most urbanized and industrialized section of the country. Undoubtedly, the Bohemian region has benefitted from its shared borders with West Germany and Austria. For those industries that require a low-cost, fairly well-educated work force that can function in an industrial environment, Bohemia can be an ideal location.

This is particularly true if the foreign investor understands the state of neglect that characterizes industrial facilities. Korean firms, having started virtually from scratch in the early 1950s, may be more tolerant of such conditions. Samsung already has invested in an outdated, abandoned factory in the Soviet Union. After teaching Soviet workers its principles of quality control, the Korean firm now realizes daily output of 1,200 video recorders from the converted facility.

In a region hungry for quality consumer durables, Samsung would find a ready market for products such as moderately priced television sets, sound systems, and microwave ovens. Nor would it be necessary to restrict output to domestic markets. The Czechoslovakian government has enacted legislative changes to make it easier for a foreign firm to do business there. Foreign concerns may hold majority ownership in enterprises, repatriate earnings in convertible currency and avoid the mandatory partial convertible currency surrender that applies to domestic enterprises.

The Moravian section of Czechoslovakia, where agriculture plays a greater role, has a more mixed economy than Bohemia. However, the fertile land has not precluded industrial development. In fact, a wide range of manufactured goods and automobiles are produced here. As is true in Bohemia, the primary problem is that these manufactures are not up to Western standards.

However, Hyundai, another Korean firm, may find that this is not an insurmountable obstacle. As living standards in the region improve, the need will arise for an affordable form of personal transportation. Hyundai appears to have remained committed to that end of the market. Moravian workers and facilities, combined with Korean innovation and quality control, may be the key to growth for all parties concerned.

The Slovakian region of Czechoslovakia holds less immediate industrial promise. With vast forests and sheep pastures, Slovakia's industrial development occurred primarily after 1945. Shipbuilding and metal processing are important components of its manufacturing sector. However, the shipbuilding industry has faced over-capacity problems worldwide for several years. Besides, with the exception of rivers flowing through the region, Moravia (indeed, the whole country) is landlocked.

These factors have contributed to a low standard of living for residents of this region. This is not to suggest that Slovakia has no place in a three-nation trading block. Its agricultural potential could be more fully exploited so that it might act as one of the most important food sources for all the more industrialized sections. Over the long-term, untapped forestry and mineral resources in Slovakia could prove commercially valuable, once investment funds were channeled in that direction.

Of course, investment funds are precisely the problem. While Czechoslovakia holds considerable industrial potential, its financial structure is not yet sufficiently developed. On the other hand, Hungary has made significant strides in the financial sector. As noted earlier, the country's central bank no longer follows the typical socialist model of a monobank, that is, one bank that issues currency, finances capital projects, and provides payments services. Since 1987, the National Bank of Hungary (NBH) has been structured only as a note-issuing (currency-issuing) institution with control over the country's money supply.

If a trading block were formed among the three countries, the NBH is clearly best qualified to set monetary policy. While Yugoslavia has a technically more developed and diverse financial infrastructure, its monetary officials have shown little or no ability to manage the country's money supply. In 1980, Yugoslavian money supply stood at 45 million dinars. In 1985, it was up to 182 million dinars. By 1989, the total was 51 billion dinars. The quasi-money supply, at 78 million dinars in 1980, grew by a factor of 2,500, to 196.7 billion in 1989.[16] Under these circumstances the observed inflation rates are understandable.

At the same time, Hungary's money supply grew from 192 billion forint in 1983 (the first year available) to 355 billion in 1989, not even doubling. Quasi-money was maintained at comparable levels.[17] As a result, Hungary's producer and consumer annual price increases averaged only 4.2 percent and 8.7 percent, respectively, during the six years ended 1988.

Sound monetary policy is not the only reason that Hungary is well suited to act as a conduit for investment in the region. In addition to the five large commercial banks, small financial institutions have developed since the early 1980s, funded primarily by large banks and government ministries, although individual enterprises also have started to show interest in investing in them. Since these small financial institutions assist their clients in the issuance of securities, provide them with risk financing, and perform factoring services, as well as make loans, they are somewhat similar to merchant banks. Accordingly, the small banks can be extremely helpful in supporting the small-scale industries that are so critical in nurturing an entrepreneurial environment.

The Hungarian bond market is also an important mechanism for industrial finance. The first Hungarian bonds were issued in 1981 by local government authorities. The list of permissible issuers has now been expanded to include the central government, financial institutions, and businesses.

As noted earlier, the Hungarian forint is tied to a basket of convertible currencies. Because of the country's strong monetary management, the currency has been relatively stable. If the values of Czechoslovakian and Yugoslavian currencies were tied to the forint and a conversion facility established in Hungary, then investment in the three-nation trading block could be greatly simplified.

While Yugoslavs can learn valuable lessons from the Hungarian banking officials, Hungarians could benefit from tutorials in the Yugoslavian self-management form of socialism. Even in the social sector, the assets of an enterprise are managed based on workers' decisions. The core of economic philosophy is not that everyone should share poverty, but that everyone should have the opportunity to become financially independent. A Yugoslav also has the option of self-employment in small-scale industries in the private sector. Up to 10 self-employed individuals can form a joint private shop. Each of these can employ up to 20 workers. Thus, private concerns with 10 owners may employ up to 200 people. Of course, owners may not violate socially acceptable norms of the treatment of workers.

Notwithstanding worker protections, Yugoslavia has a very definite market orientation. As early as 1984, Yugoslavia permitted foreign firms to own more than 49 percent of the interest of a commercial joint venture, with repatriation rights guaranteed. During the 1980s, the government emphasized export expansion and import contraction. The self-management philosophy, along with a private sector structure, contributes to a favorable business environment.

However, Yugoslavia has special problems to overcome. Croatia and Slovenia, near the Austrian border, enjoy a much higher standard of living than the most populous region of Serbia. Slovenia is the most wealthy and industrial of all Yugoslav republics. Croatia produces most of the country's coal, timber, and petroleum. On the other hand, Serbia is primarily agricultural, producing 50 percent of the nation's food supply. Even less well off is the Bosnia-Hercogovina region. The disparity in income levels among the republics has proved to be a volatile combination that threatens to split the country apart. Analysts worry that instability in Yugoslavia will precipitate violence throughout the region, as was true at the beginning of World War I. However, an even more compelling reason why these tensions must be resolved is that Yugoslavia has the most Western outlook and must participate in the region's recovery.

The reasonable solution, of course, is for each region to be better developed so as to reach its own potential. If Serbia routinely sold its agricultural output not only throughout Yugoslavia, but also throughout Hungary and Czechoslovakia, its per capita income would rise accordingly. Together, Serbia and Slovakia (Czechoslovakia) could form a food export cartel targeted for regions outside Eastern Europe.

Also, the large Serbian population is still irritated that it no longer has sovereign status. But the republic's leadership will no doubt realize, at some point, that Serbia has more to gain from economic collaboration with the rest of the country (and the region) than from isolation.

Bosnia and Hercogovina have even more to gain from a trading block among the three countries. Despite the area's rich mineral resources, roughly half of the land is forested while one-quarter is devoted to agriculture. From the perspective of goods distribution, Bosnia and Hercogovina control roughly one-half of the Yugoslavian coast line and can provide access to the rest of Eastern Europe. If exploited, the bauxite deposits along the Adriatic coast can provide an important resource in industrial development.

The catalyst in this process probably will be one or more foreign investors that can appreciate the rich mineral resources, low-cost labor, ocean access, and proximity to the more industrialized Croatia and Slovenia. Cash-rich and resource-dependent Japanese firms rank high on the list of potential investors. The auto maker Daihatsu should find that a joint venture with Yugo will securely position the firm in Eastern Europe.

Even though conditions in these three countries may worsen before they improve, it appears inevitable that each nation will begin to appreciate what it can gain from the others. Pragmatically, a nonaligned trading block will ease the transition since, while they are not part of a Soviet bloc, they are also not yet part of the capitalist West. Understanding where their strengths and weaknesses lie, Czechoslovakia, Hungary, and Yugoslavia may even move ahead at a faster pace than the former East Germany.

POLAND: A POSSIBLE PARTICIPANT

Poland could join the triad. However, if it does, it will be because Germany does not wish to be saddled with the task of reconstructing yet another former Soviet satellite. Perhaps at the core of the tension between Poland and Germany is the basic antagonism between the two peoples. Poles remember the millions of civilian lives that were taken by Germany during World War II. They also resent the unapologetic position that Germany has taken with respect to war reparations.

On the other side of the border, many Germans believe that their Polish neighbors lack a strong work ethic and condemn the quality of

Polish workmanship and the country's inefficient industrial structure. Nevertheless, Germany appears to recognize that Poland must have a stable economy in order to limit Polish immigration into Germany. Thirteen of the 25 joint ventures in Poland's service sector initiated in the first half of 1989 were with West German firms.

Poland's external debt is close to $40 billion in the East, second only to the Soviet Union. Of this, roughly one-quarter is owed to commercial banks. In 1988, West German banks held over 35 percent of Poland's bank debt. It is interesting to note that not even 16 percent of East Germany's bank debt was owed to West German institutions.

Having made such a substantial contribution to the Polish economy, continued support at these levels could be unsustainable post-reunification. So, Germany may encourage Poland's participation in a neutral trading block with other East European countries.

However, mindful that the abrupt severing of ties by the Soviet Union could be viewed by historians as opportunistic, Germany may take a different approach. One possible alternative is for Germany to make the public gesture of forgiving its portion of Polish debt. In this way, the country can receive positive publicity while distancing itself from what may be considered an economic black hole. Not insignificantly, Germany also would distance itself from further reunification-related demands from the Soviet Union.

THE ROUGH ROAD AHEAD

Even if all four countries band together, economic recovery will not be simple. Philosophical realignments are never easy. When attempted under the strain of economic uncertainty and hardship, the process is further complicated. However, if all parties look to the future instead of the past, that future may, indeed, hold much promise.

NOTES

1. Erich Honeker governed East Germany for 18 years until his resignation under pressure in 1989.
2. A metric ton of crude oil is equivalent to 7.275 barrels.
3. At the time of this writing, economic sanctions against Iraq are in place because of that country's invasion of Kuwait. As a result, oil exports from both countries have been severely curtailed.
4. The average price for a barrel of crude petroleum in 1986 was $13.82 (*International Financial Statistics*, yearbook, 1990).

5. The average price of Australian coal in 1986 was $39.27 per metric ton (*International Financial Statistics*, yearbook, 1990).

6. Major producers of wheat in 1986 were (in millions of metric tons) (*Statistical Abstract of the United States, 1989*):

Soviet Union	92.3
China	89.0
United States	56.8
Australia	17.4

7. The commercial catch of these four countries included fish, crustaceans, mollusks, and other aquatic life, but excluded whales and seals. The 1986 totals (in billions of pounds) (*Statistical Abstract of the United States, 1989*) were:

Japan	26.4
Soviet Union	24.8
China	17.6
United States	10.9

8. Meat-production figures included beef and veal, pork, and mutton and lamb slaughtered within national boundaries (in millions of metric tons) (*Statistical Abstract of the United States, 1989*):

China	19.5
United States	17.8
Soviet Union	14.4

9. Land mass (in thousands of square miles) (*Rand McNally World Atlas,* 1986) and 1988 population estimates (in millions) (*World Bank Atlas 1989*) for the four countries analyzed here are:

	Area	Population
Soviet Union	8,600	285.7
Japan	146	122.4
United States	3,679	245.9
China	3,631	1,083.9

10. The area of Siberia is approximately 3 million square miles (Levey and Greenhall, 1983).

11. Commercial vehicles in use in the USSR (1981) and China (1980) were 8,304 and 1,436, respectively, while merchant fleet

capacities were 28,556 and 18,484 deadweight tons, respectively (*Handbook of International Trade and Development Statistics 1988*).

12.   Bulgaria and Romania became independent states in 1908 and 1878, respectively.

13.   The Austrian Hapsburg Empire began in 1282 and was reorganized as the Austro-Hungarian Monarchy in 1867. The monarchy was dissolved at the end of World War I.

14.   Over half of Yugoslavia's exports ($10 to $12 billion per year) are destined for industrialized countries. By contrast, Hungary has historically shipped over half its goods to other East European countries and the Soviet Union. Czechoslovakian exports to the East have amounted to 70 percent or more of the total.

15.   The population and per capita gross national product (GNP) of each country are as follows (in millions of people and U.S. dollars, respectively) (*World Bank Atlas 1989*):

	Population	GNP
Czechoslovakia	15.6	not available
Hungary	10.6	2,460
Yugoslavia	23.6	2,680

16.   Money is defined as currency (outside banks) and demand deposits (not belonging to the central government). Quasi-money includes time, savings, and foreign deposits of all parties other than the government. In U.S. dollar terms, money supply totals were as follows (in billions) (*International Financial Statistics*):

	1980	1985	1989
Money	15.0	5.9	4.3
Quasi-money	26.0	16.8	16.6

17.   The Hungarian money supply in billions of U.S. dollars on these dates totaled (*International Financial Statistics*):

	1983	1989
Money	4.3	5.7
Quasi-money	5.2	5.6

6

The Forgotten Region of Sub-Saharan Africa: Poverty among Riches

NO HINT OF GLOBALIZATION

Sub-Saharan Africa has been least affected by waves of economic development around the world. When African colonization officially ended, other forms of hardship took its place. As the attention of the financial world is drawn toward the needs of Eastern Europe, Sub-Saharan Africa will suffer even more. It is ironic that, after decades of first plundering and then neglecting the African continent, Western European countries now appear to suggest that the reconstruction of Eastern Europe is a much more pressing need.

To make matters worse, no country fulfills the role of economic locomotive here as Japan does in Asia and Germany does in Europe. In fact, South Africans make no pretense about the disdain with which they regard Black Africans. In the North, Arabs ignore (or manipulate) religious tenets to terrorize and subjugate nonbelievers.

After independence, a system of one-party rule often replaced the colonial masters. As was true in Eastern Europe, official corruption was a not infrequent by-product. Currently, the call for increased democratization is beginning to be heard. However, democracy without economic wherewithal will not be an adequate remedy for all that ails Sub-Saharan Africa.

Instead, leaders of the region should carefully study the lessons of Europe. Even among countries with historically tense relations, common interests of economic development can be served. Individually, African countries are weak and find it difficult to compete in the world economy. Collectively, these same nations are capable of constructing a consistent, reasonable approach to foreign investment that does not serve to recolonize them. At a minimum, this means that Sub-Saharan Africa must look beyond traditional trading patterns with former European masters. With respect to needed technical assistance in such a transformation to the Western model, an alliance with African Americans could bring more sustained commitment than past endeavors with the Europeans. Dramatic changes must occur since past industrial and trade policies have done little to lift most Africans above subsistence standards of living.

THE WORLD'S POOREST REGION

Of the 175 countries of the world, 53 generated per capita income (gross national product) of less than $500 in 1987. Thirty-three of the 53 are in Sub-Saharan Africa. Most of the remaining 12 countries in this region realized per capita income of less than $1,000.[1] To illustrate the poverty that is suggested by these income levels, one need only consider the cases of Poland and Hungary. By Western standards, these two countries were in dire need of food and basic consumer goods during the late 1980s. Yet at $1,930 and $2,240, 1987 per capita GNPs in Poland and Hungary, respectively, were roughly four times as large as most in Sub-Saharan Africa.

It should be noted that 1987 did not mark the beginning of these disparities. As Table 6.1 shows, the region's aggregate GNP fell 35 percent from 1980 through 1987. In Latin America, economic conditions were severely constrained by well-publicized debt-related problems. Nevertheless, 1987 nominal GNP stood 7 percent higher than its 1980 counterpart. In developing Europe and East Asia, the increases exceeded 15 percent. There is no question that the 35 percent decline in Africa implies devastating economic conditions for this region.

Such conditions are further reflected in the level of international monetary reserves of the same developing regions, also shown in Table 6.1. One of the first observations is that the 43 countries in Sub-Saharan Africa held less than $8 billion in reserves in 1987, while the 10 developing countries of Europe held over $35 billion. The developing Latin American and East Asian regions, also with fewer nations than Africa, each held over $50 billion. The net effect is that the average African country had international reserves of about $200 million, while the average was as high as $5 billion in other regions.

TABLE 6.1
Regional Comparisons of Developing Countries — Sub-Saharan Africa, Latin America, Europe, and Asia

GNP: % change from 1980 to 1987

Sub-Saharan Africa	-35%
Latin America	7
Europe	18
East Asia	16

International Reserves: 1987 ($ billions)

	Total	# of countries	Average per country
Sub-Saharan Africa	$ 7.7	43	$ 0.2
Latin America	50.6	27	1.9
Europe	36.3	10	3.6
East Asia	65.3	13	5.0

Annual Mineral Production (billions of 1980 constant dollars)

	1970	1987
Sub-Saharan Africa	$ 6	$ 3
Latin America	8	15
Europe	n.a.	n.a.
East Asia	6	13

External Financing (billions of dollars)
From 1983 through 1984 (1) and from 1985 through 1989 (2)

	Commercial loans		Bond Issues	
	(1)	(2)	(1)	(2)
Africa	$ 4.1	$-3.7	$ 1.6	$2.2
Latin America	18.7	-9.7	0.2	2.4
Europe	-1.0	-1.6	0.7	8.8
Asia	16.9	33.6	5.1	15.8

n.a. = not available

Sources: Author's calculations based on: World Bank. *World Debt Tables, External Debt of Developing Countries*, 1988/89 ed., vol. I. (GNP and international reserves); World Bank. *Sub-Saharan Africa: From Crisis to Sustainable Growth*, 1989, p. 124 (mineral production); International Monetary Fund. *International Capital Markets, Developments and Prospects*, 1989 and 1990 (external financing).

THE PARADOX OF UNEXPLOITED MINERAL WEALTH

While Africans suffer declining incomes and occupy the ranks of the most poverty-stricken nations, large mineral deposits lie virtually untouched. Nowhere else can this degree of deprivation be observed along with so high a level of natural resource endowments. Although several countries present useful examples of this illogical situation, Ghana is a good case in point.

Currently, the country has the potential to produce an additional 1 million ounces of gold per year. In fact, at the time of Ghana's independence in 1956, production was already at the 1-million-ounce level. However, after 1956, foreign investment declined substantially, partially because of political instability. By 1983, annual gold production had fallen below 400,000 ounces a year. The government introduced more attractive incentives for foreign investment in 1986 in the hope of stimulating more interest from abroad and ultimately realizing the country's production potential.

The production output in Ghana will be tied directly to the amount of exploration that is conducted, which is, of course, related to the degree of mining investment. Unfortunately, much of the foreign investment capital that left Ghana in the 1970s was redeployed in Australia. In Australia, the 1987 cost of gold exploration alone was $280 million, or 13 percent of that year's production of $2.1 billion. In the same year, the total Sub-Saharan investment in all mineral exploration was $100 million, or 2 percent of the region's $5 billion mineral production. Thus, an additional $25 million in exploration in Ghana would not appear to be an unrealistic expectation.

The cost of an actual mine is roughly equivalent to its annual production. Since the value of 1 million ounces of gold is approximately $400 million, this also would be the cost of setting up the required mine(s) in Ghana to realize the increased annual gold production potential.

Unfortunately, such investments are not easily obtained in Sub-Saharan Africa. Ghana's overlooked opportunity is the rule rather than the exception. A major gold belt was recently discovered in southern Ethiopia, where other promising mineral deposits in the western and northern regions of the country have barely been explored. Precious metals in Sudan, Burkina Faso, and Mali are underexploited. Petroleum and non-precious metal reserves have not reached their potential in Benin and Chad. Tanzania, a major diamond producer, has hardly touched its iron ore and coal. Somalia and Malawi realize little benefit from any of their mineral resources.

Despite these ample reserves, regional mineral production has declined in real terms. As Table 6.1 also shows, Africa, Latin America, and East Asia enjoyed roughly equivalent mineral output in 1970. By 1987, Latin America and East Asia had doubled their production figures. However, Sub-Saharan Africa produced at one-half the 1970 levels. Zaire and Zambia help to illustrate this phenomenon. In these countries, the quality of copper is considered to be three to four times as high as the quality of that in North America. Nevertheless, copper production in Zaire and Zambia plummeted from 24 percent of the world total in 1960 to only 15 percent by 1987. Currently, the leading producers are Chile, the United States, and Canada.

These have not always been the trends in Africa. From the 1950s to early 1970s, mining activities attracted substantial amounts of foreign investment. However, around the time of independence (early 1960s), foreign capital began to leave the region. The time between discovery of a mineral deposit and the beginning of actual production ranges from 5 to 15 years. Thus, it was not until the 1970s that declines in mineral output began to occur.

Natural questions arise in this scenario. Why should foreign investors pull out when host countries become independent? After foreign investors leave, why would host countries not continue to develop their reserves by reinvesting export proceeds into new exploration? The answer to the first question appears to also be the answer to the second.

Foreign investors may not conduct business with an independent country in the same way that it does a colony or territory. A sovereign state generally expects to be considered a full, negotiating partner in any enterprise that operates within its borders. Apparently, the foreign investors in Africa concluded that if they were to be forced into this kind of arrangement, they would prefer to take their investment funds elsewhere. That is precisely what happened. Large copper deposits were found in Chile, base metal and tin in Brazil, bauxite in Venezuela, and industrial minerals, gold, and diamonds in Australia. During the 1980s, fully one-half of the money spent on mining exploration was devoted to the search for gold and most was invested in Australia, Canada, and the United States. Meanwhile, African gold production languished.

The failure of post-independence governments to keep exploration and production at acceptable levels may be directly attributed to the pre-independence relationships between foreign investor and host country. Since foreigners considered host countries as something less than full partners, there was little technology transfer. When the investors left the region, they took most of the technical and management expertise with them. Thus, the region was short on skills and even shorter on capital.

The observations with respect to minerals are no less applicable to fuel deposits. The region's crude petroleum output is approximately 2.2 million barrels a day, with 80 percent originating in Angola and Nigeria. Since the oil shocks of the 1970s, most other African countries have been forced to devote a large share of their export earnings to the purchase of crude.

At the same time, there may be significant oil reserves outside Angola and Nigeria. Currently, producing oil fields are concentrated around the Gulf of Guinea (Angola, Cameroon, Congo, the Ivory Coast, Gabon, and Nigeria). However, even those fields are underutilized. The natural gas by-products are flared rather than being piped for use throughout the region, because wood fuels (fuel wood, charcoal, and agricultural residues) constitute 70 percent of domestic fuel consumption. It is even believed significant non-oil natural gas reserves lie in Sudan, Tanzania, and Mozambique. However, almost no oil exploration has been conducted outside the Gulf region.

In 1987, Latin America drilled 2,300 oil wells. During the same year, the number in Sub-Saharan Africa was only 237. The difference is a factor of ten that may not be attributed to difficulty of finding oil in Africa or to high production costs. Throughout the world, the average number of wells required to find one oil deposit is 5.6. In Africa, the average is 2.5 wells. Further, once the deposit has been located, the costs of African production are competitive with those of Indonesia, the North Sea, and Alaska. With relative ease of exploration and production, why is there so little attention to the reserves of this region?

The lack of sufficient energy resources has helped to stagnate the region's economic growth. How does a region industrialize when 70 percent of its fuel is derived from wood? Even with such a high utilization of non-petroleum energy, a disproportionate share of meager export earnings is often devoted to fuel imports. For example, Benin spends 97 percent of its export earnings on fuel imports. Even though gas deposits are believed to exist in Sudan and Tanzania, fuel imports cost the two countries 38 percent and 56 percent, respectively, of annual export revenues, while countries in the Gulf region flare natural gas by-products.

Generally, the independent governments have not had sufficient capital to explore for deposits. Further, the petroleum-savvy Saudi Arabians appear to have no incentive to assist their destitute neighbor in becoming energy self-sufficient. To do so might disturb the current balance of power among energy-producing nations. It has become increasingly apparent that the 1990 conflict between Iraq, Kuwait, and Saudi Arabia was sparked partially by the desire of the Iraqi government to increase the price of oil so that wartime debt could be more easily amortized. The resistance by other oil-producing Arab countries to higher crude prices helped precipitate Iraq's invasion of Kuwait and worldwide involvement in the Persian Gulf War that followed.

Because of this preoccupation with crude oil price levels, Sub-Saharan Africa has not and will not receive any help in developing its fuel and other mineral resources from neighboring Arab countries. Nor may the socialist governments look for help from the Soviet Union. Now that the Soviets have effectively broken their economic ties with Eastern Europe, there is no reason to believe that Moscow will feel a deeper commitment to Africans than it feels to East Europeans. Likewise, West Europeans are much more concerned about the impending Single European Market and the reconstruction of Eastern Europe than with the problems of Africa, even though they helped create most of them. In the United States, the welfare of Africa remains as it has always been, that is, a non-issue.

THE WORLD'S CAPITAL ELUDES
SUB-SAHARAN AFRICA

Despite a wealth of resources in the Sub-Saharan, capital flows have systematically evaded the region. The bottom portion of Table 6.1 illustrates this point. Commercial bank loans to developing countries in 1983 and 1984 totaled $41.5 billion. Most of these commercial bank disbursements went to Latin America and to Asia for a total of $36 billion. Net loan activity in developing Europe represented a repayment of $1 billion.

Africa received slightly over $4 billion in financing during this two-year period. Of this, South Africa was the recipient of $1.6 billion in new loans. Countries in the northern section of the continent received the next largest distributions: Nigeria ($500 million), Morocco ($400 million), and Algeria ($300 million).

However, the level of commercial bank financing has since declined to all developing countries. From 1985 through September 1989, new loans to developing countries amounted to only $22 billion. That is, during this almost five-year period, net new bank financing to developing countries was about half the amount during the previous two-year period. Flows to some countries increased, while other countries made net loan repayments. Only Asia realized a net capital inflow from bank financing during the 1985 to 1989 period.

Clearly, in the wake of commercial bank retrenchment, bond issues (also shown in Table 6.1) have become a much more important source of developing-country financing. In 1983 and 1984, such bond issues amounted to $7.6 billion, with Asian countries raising 67 percent of this total. Africa was the next highest bond-issuing region with $1.6 billion. However, South Africa was the only recipient.

In the five years ended 1989, new developing-country issues totaled slightly more than $29 billion. Once again, Asian issuers represented over half the total dollar value of these bonds. However, by this time, the volume of funds generated by Latin America and Europe each outpaced total African bond issues. It is important to note that access to competitive capital markets is one of the prerequisites to modern industrialization. Given that viable projects and other opportunities exist within a capital-importing country, foreign capital market scrutiny helps to separate the efficient operations from the inefficient. To the extent that efficient projects receive financial support, the industrial fabric of the country improves.

In this regard, Africa attracted less in competitive international bond funds than other developing regions, that is, only $2.2 billion during the five years ended 1989. Of this total, Algerian and South African bonds constituted $1.3 billion and $840 million, respectively.

In essence, Sub-Saharan countries have no access to competitive commercial bank loan or bond markets. Instead, they must rely heavily on grants and concessional loans because they have been excluded from the mainstream of world business, despite the tremendous natural resources that they collectively possess. Further, the Arabs in the region have established a class system that promises to maintain the status quo.

ARAB CONTEMPT FOR BLACK AFRICANS

It seems strange that Sub-Saharan Africa should go begging for foreign investment in the 1970s when neighboring Arabs enjoyed unprecedented windfalls in crude oil profits during that decade. Saudi Arabia alone realized merchandise trade surpluses of $352 billion in the ten years from 1973 through 1982. This is almost 50 times the level of merchandise trade surpluses that the country experienced during the five years ended 1972 ($7.6 billion). While it is true that Saudi Arabia needed development itself, during the ten years noted above, the country was able to absorb only $174 billion in domestic capital formation, that is, social and industrial infrastructure. During this ten-year period, there was so much liquidity in the country's coffers that $102 billion was invested abroad in long-term bonds, stocks, and other financial instruments.

At the same time, in three neighboring African countries, Somalia, Ethiopia, and Sudan, total foreign direct and portfolio investment from all sources was less than $115 million. In Sudan, not one dollar in direct or portfolio investment was realized. It seems almost inconceivable that this country, located just across the Red Sea, or roughly 200 miles from Saudi Arabia, would not attract any investment funds from that country or anywhere else in the oil-exporting region. Yet neither the promise of unexploited mineral deposits nor a large, low-cost labor force was a sufficient inducement.

Since the Islamic faith encourages investment in productive enterprises, this is particularly perplexing. The Koran (the equivalent of the Christian Bible) contains definite provisions with respect to acceptable economic practices. One of these provisions is that interest should not be charged, that it is immoral. According to the Koran, establishing a lender's fixed return from an investment before the outcome is known with certainty shows no compassion for the borrower. If the venture does not succeed as hoped for, the borrower may be unable to completely repay interest and principal. Thus, a kind of partnership is preferable, one in which all parties share gains and losses. Within these parameters of fairness and morality, the investment function is encouraged.

However, the manner in which the Arab world has treated Black Africans cannot, in any way, be considered moral. Not only have Arabs not made prudent investments in nearby countries, but they continue to treat Black Africans as inferior beings. Beginning in the nineteenth century, Arab slave traders traveled through Sudan and captured non-Muslim Africans under the pretense that they were prisoners of war. Arab military leadership in the mid-twentieth century blocked the efforts of Christian missionaries to educate the non-Muslims in southern Sudan.

Today, Arab militia routinely kill hundreds of unarmed, non-Muslim, Sudanese civilians, particularly the Dinka people in the south, the backbone of the resistance movement against Arab leadership. As a result of this tyranny, non-Muslims often are forced to leave their villages to escape death or enslavement. Slave trading has become so common that the price for a Dinka slave dropped from $90 in 1988 to $15 in 1990.

This is not to suggest that such treatment is restricted to Sudan. The Arab government of Chad condones wide-scale civilian executions of non-Muslims. Many that are not killed are enslaved. In Mauritania, slaves are told that their service to masters is a religious duty. Of course, officially, slavery is not recognized. In fact, the most recent government pronouncement abolishing slavery came in 1980. Nevertheless, the practice continues with 400,000 of the nation's 2 million people in some form of bondage to 600,000 Arab masters.

From the Western perspective, the Arab contempt for Black Africans should not really be difficult to understand, given the arrogance of the Saudi Arabian government in its dealings with the

United States. The 1990 conflict between Iraq and Kuwait increased crude-oil prices by roughly $10 a barrel. Saudi Arabia, along with every other oil producer, realized substantial windfall profits as a result. Yet when the Saudis accepted the military support of the United States to defend its oil fields against a possible Iraqi attack, the U.S. government found it necessary to ask several countries for financial help to support the massive military buildup that was necessary.

As if that were not demeaning enough, the Saudi Arabian government forbade U.S. military personnel from practicing their chosen religious faith on Saudi territory since they were all considered infidels. Worse yet, U.S. personnel were not permitted to display the American flag. If Arabs feel comfortable treating trained military personnel from, arguably, the most powerful country in the world with such disdain, what little concern they must feel for poverty-stricken Black Africans. This, then, explains why oil-rich Arabs have been no economic locomotive in Sub-Saharan Africa.

THE EFFECTS OF LONG-TERM NEGLECT

Because of the factors noted above, industrialization in the Sub-Saharan has been slow to develop. African exports are largely composed of fuels, minerals, metals, and other primary commodities. In 1987, these categories represented 86 percent of the region's merchandise exports. Higher value-added products are simply not produced in significant quantities.

In fact, 71 percent of the 1987 work force was engaged in agriculture, much of it subsistence farming. In a number of countries, exports are primarily agricultural goods.[2] Heavy dependence on agricultural output, particularly in those countries with underutilized mineral production capabilities, has meant having to survive in the world economy by selling agricultural goods, whose prices were stable or declining, while mineral prices increased.[3]

With little external investment capital and correspondingly low industrial development, output fell in both agricultural and industrial sectors. As shown in Table 6.2, the lowest-income countries were particularly hard hit. Agricultural output dropped from $51 billion in 1980 to under $34 billion in 1987, with Nigeria accounting for the bulk of that decline. Annual manufacturing output, excluding Nigeria, was also essentially unchanged at approximately $5 billion. That is to say, the 30 poorest Sub-Saharan countries showed no increase in total nominal

TABLE 6.2
Output, Trade, and Debt in Sub-Saharan Africa

Output (billions of dollars)

Per capital GNP	# of Countries	Agriculture 1980	1987	Manufacturing 1980	1987
Under $500	31	$51.0	$33.8	$14.6	$10.5
(of which: Nigeria		26.0	7.3	9.2	5.2)
Greater than $500	12	9.5	13.7	4.2	6.1

Trade (billions of dollars)

Per capita GNP	1980 Exports	Imports	Bal.	1987 Exports	Imports	Bal.
Under $500	$ 39.1	$ 34.3	$4.8	$ 16.8	$ 22.0	$-5.2
(of which: Nigeria	26.0	16.6	9.4	7.4	7.8	-0.4)
Greater than $500	12.7	11.8	0.9	13.5	11.6	1.9

Debt (billions of dollars) and Debt to GNP

	1980 Debt	Debt/GNP	1987 Debt	Debt/GNP
Sub-Saharan Africa	$ 56.0	0.282	$128.8	1.001
Latin America	242.6	0.353	442.5	0.601
Europe	94.9	0.289	202.1	0.521
East Asia	90.5	0.172	206.3	0.338

Sources: Author's calculations based on: World Bank. *Sub-Saharan Africa: From Crisis to Sustainable Growth*, 1989, pp. 224, 236, 240 (output and trade); World Bank. *World Debt Tables, External Debt of Developing Countries*, 1988/89 ed., vol. I (debt).

output from 1980 through 1987. When inflation is considered, the net effect is that real output declined.

The 12 countries with per capita GNP above $500 manufactured $2 billion more in 1987 than in 1980. However, at a $6 billion total, this is an average of only $500 million each. In no way can this level of total industrial production sustain these developing countries.

The external trade figures (also in Table 6.2) verify this observation. In 1980, the entire region exported goods valued at $52 billion, of which Nigeria contributed $26 billion (mostly crude oil). Even so, excluding Nigeria, the aggregate trade balance was a deficit of $3.7 billion. Seven years later, the trade balance was essentially the same except that in 1987 even Nigeria ran a small deficit. However, the cost of containing this deficit has been high. While the 12 nations above a $500 per capita GNP held both exports and imports steady, the low-income countries reduced total external trade (exports and imports) by over $7 billion or 23 percent in nominal terms.[4]

The deteriorating condition of domestic output and international trade can only mean that the desperate situation in Sub-Saharan Africa will get worse. That is even clearer, given the amount of debt that the region has had to assume. Oil price increases in the 1970s began the process of chronic trade disequilibria and slumping agricultural commodity prices further aggravated the situation. In 1980, external debt was 28 percent of Sub-Saharan GNP (see Table 6.2). At the time, this was actually lower than the ratios in Europe and Latin America. However, with no access to capital markets for investment funds, the region has piled up a mountain of official debt (both bilateral and multilateral) just to stay afloat.[5]

During the seven years that followed, the debt burden of Latin America was hotly debated in the United States as commercial banks grappled with the possibility (now a probability) that their loans to Latin America might not be repaid. These are certainly very serious problems for both lenders and borrowers, particularly since Latin American debt went from 35 percent of GNP in 1980 to 60 percent in 1987.

Yet, if the debt burden in Latin America is critical (and it certainly is), then how does one describe the African situation? By 1987, African debt was over 100 percent of GNP. With declining real output, slumping exports, and mounting debt, the region has been forced to seek more and more grants. In other words, it has become even more dependent on the world's charity.

OVER-RELIANCE ON OFFICIAL
FINANCIAL RESOURCES

In general, developing countries may receive either official or private external financial support. In the broad category of official financial flows are included official development assistance (ODA) and "other" official flows. ODA is any concessional payment made by a government to another country that is intended to assist in the economic development of the recipient country and that has a grant component of at least 25 percent. Other official flows are those from a government to another country that do not meet one or the other of these two criteria. Accordingly, other official flows are nonconcessional. Export credits represent a large portion of such nonconcessional official flows.

Without official payments from industrialized governments, Sub-Saharan Africa would find itself in an even more desperate condition. The top portion of Table 6.3 shows total financial flows to developing regions by DAC members, DAC-financed multinational organizations, and OPEC contributors from 1983 through 1986.[6] During this period, Sub-Saharan countries received almost $50 billion from these sources, with 65 percent attributable to bilateral arrangements with DAC members. The shares of Latin American and North African bilateral receipts from DAC were even higher at 80 percent and 81 percent,

TABLE 6.3
Financial Flows to Developing Countries (1), 1983-1986

Financial flows by region

	Total (2)	% of Total			Per capita (in dollars)	
		DAC funds				
		BL	MN	OPEC funds	Flows	GDP (3)
Latin America	$ 84.0	79.7%	20.2%	0.1%	$ 203	$1,822
North Africa	19.9	80.8	16.6	2.6	192	1,370
Sub-Sah. Africa	49.5	64.6	29.3	6.1	114	372
West Asia	18.1	39.0	18.9	42.1	114	2,733
Other Asia	58.4	60.8	32.2	7.0	40	489

Selected recipients of OPEC financial flows

	Financial flows		1986
	Total (4)	Per capita	Per capita GDP
West Asia:			
Syria	$2,825	$ 258	$1,744
Jordan	2,190	597	1,355
Yemen	712	87	451
Bahrain	535	1,188	8,177
Oman	264	206	5,731
Democratic Yemen	211	89	403
North Africa:			
Tunisia	482	67	1,222
Morocco	251	11	657
Algeria	301	13	2,713
Sub-Saharan Africa:			
Sudan	696	31	382
Mauritania	243	125	413
Senegal	167	25	564
Somalia	142	26	351
Mali	121	14	188

Notes: (1) financial flows include bilateral loans and grants and financing through multinational organizations; (2) billions of dollars; (3) 1986 gross domestic product; (4) millions of dollars; DAC = Development Assistance Committee (OECD); BL = bilateral; MN = multinational organizations.

Sources: Author's calculations based on: United Nations. *Handbook of International Trade and Development Statistics, 1988.* New York: United Nations, 1989; United Nations. *Financial Solidarity for Development: Development Assistance from OPEC Members and Institutions to Other Developing Countries 1982–1986, 1988 Supplement.* New York: United Nations, 1988.

respectively. However, the ODA, or concessional, payments to Sub-Saharan countries constituted almost one-half of the total $50 billion. Other regions received more official export credits and private financing.[7]

The Sub-Saharan is also heavily dependent on DAC-financed multinational organizations and agencies for external financing (29 percent of the total). Again, most of this is also concessional in nature. Only 6 percent of the total was received from OPEC members or organizations. Table 6.3 also illustrates how generally dependent the region is on external finance. Total financial flows from such sources amounted to $114 per capita during the four-year period. This was fully 31 percent of 1986 per capita gross domestic product (GDP). In no other region was this ratio so high.[8]

It is interesting that West Asia received the same amount of per capita financial support as the Sub-Saharan even though its per capita GDP was over seven times as high. In fact, West Asia had a higher average GDP than any other developing region. And 42 percent of the West Asian funds originated from OPEC members. Since the geographic region of West Asia includes all the OPEC members except Nigeria and Venezuela, approximately half of OPEC financial assistance to developing countries was kept in the Arabs' own back yard.[9] Some of the larger recipients of OPEC assistance (also in Table 6.3) were Syria, Jordan, Yemen, Bahrain, Oman, and Democratic Yemen. All but one of these shares a border with Saudi Arabia. Not coincidentally, Saudi Arabia is the major provider of OPEC financial assistance.[10]

Essentially, Saudi Arabia is using so-called aid to developing countries to strengthen its own fortress within the region. There can be little other explanation when OPEC provides Bahrain with $1,188 per capita when its GDP is $8,177, but provides only $31 per person in Sudan where the income is $382.

While the per capita amount paid to the small country of Bahrain appears completely out of line, the aggregate payments to Syria and Jordan suggest a rather interesting relationship. Of the total $24 billion disbursed to developing countries by OPEC members and organizations from 1983 through 1986, $5 billion (20 percent) found its way to Syria and Jordan. No other recipient was the beneficiary of so much OPEC generosity. Could it be that moderate Saudi Arabia is secretly helping to bankroll some of the international terrorists that it publicly condemns? Truthfully, it requires no great leap in logic to move from justifying slavery on religious principle to justifying terrorism for the same reason.

Whatever the nature of Arab relations, the people of Sub-Saharan Africa cannot depend on them or anyone else to solve their worsening problems. Just as the Germans and the Japanese looked to their particular competitive advantages and built their economies on strength, Africans must now do the same.

THE NEED FOR REAL CHANGE

The signals that a dramatic change will be necessary are beginning to be heard. Both traditional exports and financial assistance are threatened. The European Community (EC) is the destination of the majority of Sub-Saharan exports. The Lome Conventions accorded all ACP (African, Caribbean, and Pacific) members of the conventions duty-free access to EC markets. As the Single European Market of 1992 takes form, historical preferences certainly will be questioned. With respect to other forms of official financial aid, the need for investment funds for Eastern Europe and the Soviet Union will tend to put greater, rather than fewer, restrictions on fund allocations.

In 1980, 45 percent of all exports from developing Africa was destined for the EC. By 1986, the percentage had grown to 58 percent. As noted above, a large percentage of these exports are primary commodities, either fuel, minerals, or agricultural products. All of these categories will be affected by changes in European commerce as a result of the Single European Market.

It appears likely that EC fuel imports from the Soviet Union and Eastern Europe will increase, given the relaxation of regional tensions. African fuel exporters — Gabon, Angola, Nigeria, Guinea, and Cameroon — could be adversely affected. Should the EC adopt the EC Commission recommendation to reduce the use of cadmium-rich phosphates, exports from Senegal and Togo would suffer.

Perhaps even more potentially devastating are changes in the rules governing agricultural products. If Sub-Saharan sugar and bananas are subject to the same tariffs as those from other non-ACP countries, exports from the Ivory Coast, Cameroon, and Zimbabwe will no longer enjoy preferential status. If the maximum tar content for EC cigarettes is reduced, as the Commission has also recommended, tobacco producers Malawi and Zimbabwe could face real challenges. Should the harmonization of standards for chocolate increase the permissible level of vegetable oil used by French and Belgian producers, the cocoa and butter exports of Ghana, Togo, Ivory Coast, Cameroon, and Nigeria would decline.

Not only is the traditionally largest market for African exports now substantially less secure, but the climate is also changing for the kind of official aid upon which the region is so dependent. At the July 1990 economic conference of Western leaders, the portion of the agenda allocated for foreign aid discussions focused on the Soviet Union, not Sub-Saharan Africa. At the same time, the push for pluralist governments in Europe has spilled over to Africa, at least in the minds of Western officials responsible for aid allocations. The message appears to be that, without more democratic governments, the level of aid will be reduced. This is, of course, not the message to developing Europe. European countries stand to receive more aid if they satisfactorily democratize. African nations will receive less aid if they do not.

Setting aside the less-than-evenhanded manner in which the democratization issue is being handled, the transition to a more pluralistic government is usually not a neat and orderly process, as individual factions vie for power. Essentially, the Sub-Saharan is being pressured to take politically risky steps under the threat of being cut off from financial aid.

However, instead of viewing these developments as even more burdens to bear, the people of Africa should consider them blessings in disguise. Frankly, the financial aid has helped make the region weaker, not stronger. As an example, the advice from multinational organizations to concentrate on more efficient farming has brought unemployment to many rural farmers. Years of donor-initiated austerity programs have only led to declining income levels. Price supports from the EC have encouraged more dependence on special treatment rather than more concentration on the need to become competitive on a worldwide basis.

Looking beyond past colonial masters and comparative economic weaknesses, the region should concentrate on its strengths, that is, its resources and its people. Building on these, the Sub-Saharan countries should look for trade partners around the world with whom a mutually beneficial economic relationship can be formed.

A STRATEGY BUILT ON STRENGTH
RATHER THAN WEAKNESS

A common cliché advises that there is strength in numbers. As is true with most clichés, there is a certain amount of truth here. The peoples of Sub-Saharan Africa can no longer afford the luxury of isolation and divisiveness. While much energy has been spent analyzing and debating their differences, much less time has been devoted to considering their similarities. Common to all is the need for economic development and exploitation of abundant natural resources. An inventory of these resources would quickly convince a collective African alliance that they are among the richest peoples in the world. It also would become abundantly clear that they do not need charity. Rather, they need technical assistance to manage their endowments.

The needed assistance, however, will not come from Europe because Europeans will continue to regard Africans with condescension. The master/slave psyche is too well entrenched at this point. A reasonable working relationship with Arabs is not possible since they make no attempt to conceal their true feelings about Black Africans. For obvious reasons, joint ventures with South Africa also hold little promise.

On the other hand, people of African descent from other regions of the world will feel more of an affinity for Sub-Saharans. The one common thing that Africans and African descendants share universally is racial and economic discrimination. The ways in which they differ are precisely those attributes that could enable them to realize operational synergies in an international trade network.

With nearly 60 percent of Sub-Saharan exports headed for EC countries in 1987, the value of these exports was approximately $18 billion (since total exports were $30 billion). Only $4 billion was shipped to the United States and $900 million to all of Latin America.[11] Yet the United States, the Caribbean, and Brazil have sizeable populations of African descent. Accordingly, these markets hold considerable potential for the embryonic manufacturing sector of Africa.

In 1987 in the United States alone, more than 7 million African American families earned a total income of $167 billion. With an appropriate trade network, it appears reasonable that the Sub-Saharan could at least replicate its level of European sales in the United States. Yet, such an arrangement could impact African trade in a much more profound manner than by simply providing a larger market for existing goods (although this is no insignificant consideration).

The key to real success would be to elicit the technical help of African Americans and others who have access to an advanced educational system, but have been unable to realize their full potential because of racial intolerance. Specifically, in the United States, whites outnumber blacks by a ratio of 7 to 1. However, the number of whites with four years of college or more is 15 times the corresponding number of blacks. Reflecting both these educational disparities and societal prejudices, the number of whites earning an annual income of $35,000 or more is 23 times the number of blacks in this income category.

Thus, there is a large pool of underutilized talent in the African-American community. This talent can be the key to unleashing the economic power of Sub-Saharan Africa. By tapping the knowledge of some of the more than 100,000 African-American architects, engineers, and mathematical and computer scientists, the region can be joined in a network of roads and state-of-the-art telecommunications that would facilitate resource management, the manufacturing process, domestic and external distribution, and policy coordination.[12]

It would no longer be necessary for Nigeria to depend on a foreign concern to refine its oil. A black-owned oil company could easily be organized as a U.S./Nigerian joint venture. The Zambian textile industry would not have to confine itself primarily to military and airline uniforms, but could begin to produce a fuller range of clothing for newly established export markets and, as income levels rose, for the rest of the continent.[13] The 5,000 craftsmen of the Suame Magazine in Ghana that have worked with scrap material and primitive tools to keep 80 percent of the country's motor vehicles in operation could begin to design automobiles especially designed for driving conditions in Africa. The highly successful cookstove project in Niger could be expanded to manufacture for all the continent, immediately reducing the consumption of fuel woods, and expand to other forms of household appliance manufacture.[14] Botswana would not have to depend on DeBeers to market its diamonds but could instead collaborate in the establishment of its own wholesale and retail jewelry operations in the United States and Brazil. Zimbabwe could expend its fledgling securities market to attract and distribute capital throughout the region and abroad.

These possibilities are but a sample of the ways in which existing operations can be expanded. Other enterprises in the neglected mining sector and more advanced technologies also can be undertaken. The combination of technology, experience, capital, and low-cost labor can achieve real synergies for all partners.

Of course, the Sub-Saharan has social problems that demand immediate attention. Housing, health care, and education must be improved in order to give the populace a fighting chance to develop their natural resources. Here too, African Americans can offer critical assistance. In the United States, black social scientists, urban planners, health-care professionals, and educators number over half a million.[15] There is simply no lack of talent to help Sub-Saharan Africa find a cure for all that ails it.

Turning to the question of motivation, why should these people of African descent assume the monumental task of helping to raise the standard of living for members of an African alliance? The answer is simple. They would do it because such a combination perfectly matches the needs of each group. African Americans and others of African descent have virtually infinite management and technological skills that remain pent-up, for the most part, because they have been denied access to the natural endowments of their respective lands. Sub-Saharan Africans are starved for the knowledge that is necessary to develop the wealth that lies dormant all around them.

NO OTHER CHOICE

Under present circumstances, the future of the Sub-Saharan appears uncertain at best. Yet perhaps it really is darkest before the dawn. If this region learns the lessons offered by history in other regions of the world, all is certainly not lost. National sovereignty and independence are noble concepts, but the realities of world economics mandate a strong regional response. Sub-Saharans cannot change the rest of the world, but only strive to survive under the rules that prevail. Indeed, if a well-structured African alliance is formed and executed, the region that is now the object of pity and disdain may someday be able to vigorously compete in the arena of world commerce.

NOTES

1. In Botswana ($1,050), Mauritius ($1,490), Gabon ($2,700), and Seychelles ($3,120), 1987 per capita GNP exceeded $1,000 (*Sub-Saharan Africa*, 1989).

2. The following countries are particularly dependent on agricultural exports (*Sub-Saharan Africa*, 1989):

Country	% of Exports from agriculture	Commodities
Benin	> 50	Cocoa, cotton, palm oil
Ethiopia	> 50	Coffee
Chad	54	Cotton
Sudan	38	Cotton
Malawi	> 83	Tea, tobacco, sugar
Tanzania	56	Coffee, cotton, and tobacco
Ghana	46	Cocoa

3. The prices of Sub-Saharan agricultural exports generally peaked in the late 1970s, while primary metal prices have held up much better. Below are the ratios of 1989 price to 1975 price for seven agricultural products that are important for the region and six basic metals (*International Financial Statistics*, yearbook, 1990). (Note that a ratio of 2.0 implies that the nominal price of the associated commodity has doubled.)

Agricultural Products		*Metals*	
Cocoa	0.9970	Gold	2.3678
Cotton	1.4246	Copper	2.3021
Palm oil	0.8338	Iron ore	1.1578
Coffee	1.2596	Lead	1.7800
Tea	1.4558	Nickel	2.9126
Tobacco	1.6801	Zinc	1.9938
Sugar	0.6230		

4.   In 1980, trade of low-income countries totaled $73.4 billion, of which $42.6 billion was attributable to Nigeria. By 1987, the total was down to $38.8 billion, with Nigeria contributing $15.2 billion. Thus, non-Nigerian trade declined from $30.8 billion to $23.6 billion.

5.   In 1987, Sub-Saharan Africa owed 57 percent of its external debt to official creditors. In Europe (37 percent), Asia (35 percent), and Latin America (22 percent), the percentages were much lower (*World Debt Tables*, 1988–89).

6.   DAC is an acronym for Development Assistance Committee of the Organization for Economic Cooperation and Development. DAC members are Australia, Austria, Belgium, Canada, Denmark, Finland, France, Germany, Ireland, Italy, Japan, the Netherlands, New Zealand, Norway, Sweden, Switzerland, the United Kingdom, and the United States.

7.   The proportion of ODA in North African funds was the next highest at 41 percent. Latin American (14 percent), West Asian (13 percent), and other Asian (29 percent) bilateral receipts contained lower proportions of concessional moneys from DAC members (*Handbook of International Trade and Development Statistics 1988*).

8.   The remaining ratios are as follows:

Latin America	11%
North Africa	14%
West Asia	4%
Other Asia	8%

9.   The OPEC percentages in Table 6.3 imply total financial support to the regions shown of $15.3 billion from 1983 through 1986. Of this total, almost $8 billion was allocated to West Asia.

10.   From 1983 through 1986, Saudi Arabia contributed $18 billion of the $24 billion OPEC payments to all developing countries, including those not reflected in Table 6.3.

11.   Exports from developing Africa to the United States and Latin America were 13 percent and 3 percent, respectively, of the total.

12.   In 1987, the numbers of African Americans employed in these fields were (*Statistical Abstract of the United States, 1989*):

Architects	3,000
Engineers	60,600
Mathematical and computer scientists	45,900

13.   Substantial textiles capacity already exists in the Caribbean, but remains underutilized despite trade preferences under the U.S. Caribbean Basin Initiative (CBI). The primary constraint appears to be the requirement that raw materials (textiles) must be manufactured and cut in the United States in order for Caribbean apparel to qualify for CBI preferences.

14.   In the first two years of the program 40,000 efficient cookstoves were manufactured, representing 200 percent of planned production. Fuel-wood consumption in Niger dropped 30 percent and the 116 metalsmiths who were trained in the process doubled their normal profits (*Sub-Saharan Africa*, 1989).

15.   In 1987, the following numbers of African Americans were employed in the professions indicated (*Statistical Abstract of the United States*, 1989):

Social scientists and urban planners	18,328
Physicians	19,018
Dentists	3,360
Nurses	122,276
University and college professors	30,406
Other educators	337,178

7

Rethinking U.S. Business and Regional Economics

LESSONS FOR THE UNITED STATES

As global patterns of development and trade relations appear less likely to materialize and regional pockets of prosperity develop instead, the United States will find itself in an escalating struggle to maintain what was once the highest standard of living in the world. From the federal government to the automobile industry to the retailing sector to the heart of the country's largest cities, signs of decay are already evident. In some ways, many U.S. bureaucracies are as inflexible as the Soviet versions. If the United States is to continue to grow, indeed, if living standards are not to decline more than they have already, several lessons cannot be avoided.

The first lesson is that no institution can safely be considered a sacred cow, subject to no critical evaluation and/or modification. Another is that attempting nontraditional approaches to solve nontraditional problems is not radical, but is rational and logical. The last is that innovation has been, and will continue to be, the key to the American way of life.

Along these lines, small business enterprises must develop into more than just by-products of the sector of large corporations. Small firms must lead the way to economic adjustment, introducing even more new products and services, including automobiles and high-tech, value-added items. It is from these firms that the most significant innovations will spring. Accordingly, it is these firms that must be nurtured.

For their part, unions will be forced to abandon historically adversarial positions vis-à-vis management and use talents and resources available to them to manufacture goods that complement output of major corporations. In short, union members must assume more responsibility for their economic fate.

Of course, this will be no less true for the country as a whole. After the basic truth of self-determination is acknowledged, one of the next realizations must be that meaningful U.S. economic growth that is based solely on the domestic market is no longer feasible. Saturated product markets at home and stagnant real wage gains for a large share of the U.S. populace mean that smaller firms must join large corporations in more challenging, but potentially more fruitful, export markets.

Local governments, particularly large cities, also will be unable to escape the new realities of American life. City governments can no longer subsidize their own decline by facilitating the flight of corporations and middle- and upper-income families to suburbia. City governments cannot avoid the necessity to restructure the pricing of their goods and services in such a way as to render life within the city more appealing and life outside city limits less convenient. In short, the city is no less a corporate entity than General Motors. Its shareholders are the residents of the city and its mission is to strive for long-term viability.

One critical element of such viability is the use of the most up-to-date technology that is available to assure efficiency of service delivery and resource management. It is interesting that most Americans readily agree that the Soviet non-military industrial infrastructure, much of which dates back to the 1917 Russian Revolution, must be updated if the Soviets are to survive economically. At the same time, there appears to be little urgency to address the issue of the infrastructure of most major U.S. cities that, in many cases, is just as old and in need of technological innovation. To break this cycle, new experimental cities must be designed and implemented to meet today's challenges in the provision of government services.

THE HANDWRITING ON THE WALL

Admittedly, measures such as these are not from the same mold as most of American economic history. Yet that is precisely why they are needed. The old mold has cracked and, along with it, the American mystique of superiority and world domination. The proverbial handwriting is on the wall. We see it when we examine the automobile industry. "What's good for General Motors is good for America" was once the refrain. By 1991, this corporate symbol of America had resorted to media advertisements that implored consumers to reconsider General Motors (GM) since it, once again, produced high-quality output. The firm had fallen from a position of "standard of excellence" to one from which it was forced to apologize for the poor quality of its output.

Why such a shift? GM took its previous position for granted and, in the process, its customers. Quality control declined, leading to consumer discontent. In addition, the Cadillacs at the high end of the price spectrum looked like slightly reworked mid-sized Buicks and Chevrolets (at the middle and lower points of the price range) and were not worth their premium price. A massive reorganization in the mid-1980s did nothing to inspire the design and introduction of new, more competitive models.

The net result of these ill-advised strategic developments is that the GM share of U.S. auto sales declined from 46 percent in 1980 to 35 percent by 1989. Eleven production facilities had shut down permanently with more slated for closure. Most of the GM market share was conceded to Japanese auto makers, who by 1990, sold almost one-third of all cars purchased annually in the United States. Even with plant closings, factory utilization of the "Big Three" U.S. automobile manufacturers was down to 70 percent, while foreign firms in the United States operated at 89 percent of capacity.[1]

The signs of trouble also appear among some of the largest retailing chains. The debt burden that was brought on by waves of leveraged buyouts in the 1980s has become too heavy for many chains to carry. In 1990, 8 percent and 14 percent of sales revenues of the Allied and Federated groups, respectively, went to service debt, forcing both to seek protection from creditors through bankruptcy proceedings.

J.C. Penney revamped its product offerings to emphasize fashion apparel in an attempt to shed its image as a nondescript household merchandiser. Its shift to high fashion drew the praises of industry analysts, that is, until the U.S. economy and demand for high fashion cooled, leaving Penney with sales declines even as other basic merchandisers fared much better.

Sears Roebuck hit a plateau of sales growth during the 1980s and also decided to change its image. National brands were introduced to supplement the traditional house brands and "everyday low pricing" became the watchword. However, even with a media blitz designed to introduce and promote these major changes, sales were so disappointing that the company announced the layoff of over 20,000 employees early in 1991.

The news of employee layoffs and financial distress is not limited to auto makers and retailers. In late 1990 and early 1991, state and municipal governments faced budgets in severe deficit at the same time that demand for services increased. The $20 million deficit of the city of Los Angeles necessitated a seven-month police hiring freeze. The states of New York, New Jersey, Pennsylvania, Massachusetts, and Virginia, and the District of Columbia each expected deficits in excess of $200 million.[2]

The new mayor of the District of Columbia (elected in 1990) promised to eliminate 2,000 jobs as part of her campaign platform of reform. Observers estimated that as many as 6,000 job cuts were in order. Approximations of the required number of terminations in the city of New York alone approached 18,000. The city of Philadelphia struggled to meet payrolls as available short-term financing dried up. Meanwhile, developments in the private sector of these cities and states increased the rate of homelessness and hunger in environments of rising crime and shrinking tax bases.

The net effect of these and other developments is that, in October and November 1990, almost 500,000 jobs in all industrial sectors were lost. Over the two-year period ended December 1990, over 750,000 jobs in the manufacturing sector alone were terminated. During the 1980s, real wages in all but the export sector declined. Clearly, traditional methods of doing business will not reverse these trends.

THE IMPORTANCE OF THE SMALL FIRM

As the large firms in corporate America have restructured and downsized, employment growth in the past decade has originated overwhelmingly within small businesses. Already, over 50 percent of the work force is employed in firms composed of less than 500 individuals, with 35 percent in enterprises of fewer than 100. And the glamour of the large firm is wearing thin. Product engineering appears to have given way to balance sheet engineering as unprecedented debt levels force more and more belt-tightening. The tyranny of short-term profits often seems more powerful than the quest for service improvements.

These trends have not gone unnoticed by the U.S. labor force. In 1989, the confidence with which employees viewed senior management fell to a six-year low.[3] Of course, these feelings are understandable since hourly workers have been fortunate when they realized pay increases that more than offset the rate of inflation. At the same time, the compensation for chief executive officers (CEOs) tripled during the 1980s. By 1990, the average CEO of a firm with sales in excess of $250 million earned $633,000, 70 percent more than his counterpart in

Germany. In the United States, it is not uncommon for a CEO to earn 100 times the wage of the hourly worker. On the other hand, this ratio is rarely higher than 15 in Germany or Japan.

With this striking inequity in the distribution of worker vis-à-vis CEO compensation, the average worker should at least be assured of reasonable job security within the large corporation. Unfortunately, this has not been the case, as the job losses noted above would indicate. Nevertheless, CEOs appear to be more than capable of structuring their own financial security, not necessarily through making the firm stronger and more competitive.

Management-led takeovers in the form of leveraged buyouts (LBOs) have certainly not been an unqualified success, despite the fact that management was theoretically supposed to be able to do a better job without the threat of hostile takeover. LBOs have commonly been accompanied by asset sales and substantial employee layoffs, but not cuts in management compensation. Meanwhile, it has become increasingly apparent that the debt burden placed on many of these firms was not sustainable under any circumstances.

Even in those firms that have succumbed to hostile takeovers, golden parachutes have prevented most CEOs from facing the kind of economic hardship forced upon the average worker. In some cases, CEOs actually can emerge from a takeover in better financial condition. For example, if a CEO with annual compensation of $500,000 receives a golden parachute of $5 million, the investment earnings from such a generous severance package can give him financial security for the rest of his life. With such perverse incentives, large corporations cannot be considered the primary source of widespread future economic growth.

A small firm with less of a bureaucratic structure offers a better opportunity for both economic advancement and creativity. In fact, the extent to which small business dominates job creation appears to be positively correlated with average personal income levels. From 1976 through 1986, in those 10 U.S. states with the lowest per capita personal income, only 25 percent of new jobs originated in firms with less than 100 employees. By contrast, in higher-income states, over 40 percent of new jobs were created by small firms.[4]

However, small firm investment and activity to date has not been sufficient to effectively compete with Japan and Germany. The United States lags behind both countries in terms of capital expenditure. From 1980 through 1989, Germany and Japan plowed 20 percent and 29 percent of GNP, respectively, into capital formation. In the United States, the figure was only 17 percent.[5]

One of the consequences of this lower level of investment is that advances such as flexible manufacturing systems (FMS) have essentially eluded the small firm. FMS technology enables a manufacturer to generate more finished products on one production line, doubling and, in some cases, tripling efficiency. The time required to introduce a new product can be reduced by as much as 90 percent, while the percentage of defective output drops. Despite the obvious benefits for a small firm, ironically, in the United States, only larger outfits have invested in FMS. This is not the case in Japan, where firms can produce an average of 240 products. In the United States, the average is 25 products.

THE NEED FOR A NEW SMALL CAR MANUFACTURER

The time has come to recognize that large corporations have not served this country well. With their focus on something other than the American consumer, most of them have forgotten who their customers are, with the guiltiest of these perhaps being the Big Three auto makers. While GM, Ford, and Chrysler moved their attention to financial services diversification and foreign auto company acquisitions, these firms neglected the business of building better cars more efficiently. This is not an insignificant issue. In 1985 (see Table 4.7), worldwide exports of road motor vehicles were valued at $149 billion, second only to crude petroleum. Yet, the price of a new car is now beyond the reach of many Americans.

Table 7.1 shows that 19 percent of all nongovernment employees work in retail trade for less than $10,000 a year. Another 26 percent are employed in 15 non-trade services earning an average of less than $16,000. When the 5 percent that work in finance, insurance, and real estate are added to these, we have 50 percent of the labor force working for less than $20,000 a year.

At the same time, even an economy car can cost more than $10,000. Excluding the cost of insurance and gasoline, financing $10,000 for four years can result in monthly payments of over $250.[6] When gasoline and insurance are added to these required payments, the total monthly cost to operate a $10,000 economy model is at least $350.[7] For those retail trade workers noted above, this is 57 percent of their bring-home pay, leaving only $264 a month to cover rent, food, clothing, and other expenses.[8] Even for the relatively higher-paid nonsupervisory workers in finance, insurance, and real estate, an "economy" car payment leaves less than $800 for other necessities. While it may be tempting to assume that two of these workers support every family, such is not the case. In

TABLE 7.1

Average Earnings of Production and Nonsupervisory Workers, 1989

Industry	# of Workers (1)	Annual Earnings (2)	% of total employees (3) Industry	Workforce
Mining	519	$29,244	71.9%	0.6%
Construction	4,127	26,349	77.9	4.5
Manufacturing	13,375	22,322	68.2	14.7
Transportation public utilities	4,755	25,754	83.4	5.2
Wholesale trade	5,017	20,565	80.5	5.5
Retail trade	17,326	9,829	88.5	19.1
Finance, insurance, and real estate	4,938	17,865	72.5	5.4
Services	23,479	15,918	87.3	25.8

Notes: (1) thousands of workers; (2) average annual pre-tax earnings per capita; (3) work force totals exclude government employees.

Sources: Number of workers and earnings: *Survey of Current Business*. Washington, D.C.: U.S. Department of Commerce, Bureau of Economic Analysis, August 1990, pp. S–10 through S–12. Percentages, author's calculations based on: *Survey of Current Business*. Washington, D.C.: U.S. Department of Commerce, Bureau of Economic Analysis, August 1990, pp. S–10 through S–12.

fact, 50 percent of all U.S. families have an after-tax income of less than $20,000.[9]

In the face of these stark realities, it is amazing that U.S. auto makers appear at a loss to understand why they have lost market share. Why is it so hard to understand that, as higher-paying manufacturing jobs have been eliminated in this country to take advantage of lower-cost labor abroad, the jobs available to former factory workers do not provide the wherewithal to purchase $15,000 to $20,000 automobiles? This is not even to address the issue that the value of the car typically declines faster than the balance of the loan that is required to finance it.

Further, the aging of the American population means that there is a good number of older consumers buying new higher-priced cars. Many of these either have realized long-term capital gains from real estate holdings (often the primary residence) or have substantial pension incomes from former manufacturing employment. However, auto makers cannot rely on these demographics indefinitely since younger workers can less frequently afford to purchase a home and will not have the same average level of fringe benefits in this new service economy.

Of course, U.S. auto makers often bemoan the fact that they cannot make a profit on small cars. Where were the captains of industry when

Japanese auto makers secured a firm grip on the U.S. market by selling small, well-built cars that won the loyalty of American consumers, even as corresponding U.S. models became standing jokes? Now, with the exception of GM's Saturn, domestic car makers depend on Japanese partners to engineer and/or produce their small car offerings.

In analyzing the industry, several deficiencies are readily apparent. In the U.S. manufacturing sector in general, the ratio of managers to production and nonsupervisory workers is too high. Shown also in Table 7.1, manufacturing workers represent only 68 percent of total manufacturing employees. This means that 32 percent are in some sort of supervisory capacity. Essentially, there is one supervisor for every two workers. This is the highest percentage of any of the nongovernment industries. At the other end of the spectrum, in retail trade, there are almost eight hourly and nonsupervisory workers for every supervisor.[10] If an auto maker could reduce the bureaucratic layers, this would increase the probability that a small car could be manufactured profitably.

In addition, because the auto industry has neglected the business of building cars, it takes more time and more capital to build a U.S. car. The average model cycle of an American car is eight years, compared with four for the average Japanese car. An American production line stretches for almost a mile and a half (7,600 feet). The relatively minor Japanese manufacturer, Suzuki, has reduced this to roughly half a mile (2,600 feet). Because of the greater commitment of time and facilities, the average production run must be twice as long in the United States as in Japan.[11] The result has been fewer new models and fewer innovations on existing models.

Nevertheless, the key to Japanese success is not mysticism; it is technology. By using computer-aided design and manufacturing, Japanese auto makers can completely eliminate the plastic mock-up phase of model development, moving directly from drafting to metal prototype. Of course, production personnel and suppliers are included in the drafting stage. In fact, suppliers are pressured to minimize costs in their own shops, that is, they are strongly encouraged to use high-tech methods. Once models are developed, a Japanese line using flexible manufacturing systems can produce up to eight different models without retooling. A Detroit factory line cannot produce even four.

The technology exists to profitably manufacture a small car and the need is clear. As noted above, 50 percent of the working population faces real difficulty when attempting to purchase a new car. This is not a temporary condition. The average loss of income that has been observed in the 1980s will continue to worsen if meaningful value-added

TABLE 7.2
Job Growth by Industry, 1976–1986

Industry	% of Nongovernment jobs 1986	% of Nongovernment jobs 1976	Number of new jobs
Agriculture	1.0%	1.0%	246,954
Mining	1.2	1.4	149,815
Construction	5.5	6.1	839,188
Manufacturing	25.1	30.5	1,841,999
Transportation public utilities	6.8	7.1	1,293,362
Wholesale trade	6.9	6.9	1,549,302
Retail trade	18.8	19.0	4,031,609
Finance, insurance, and real estate	7.8	7.2	2,106,523
Services	26.9	20.8	10,210,520
Total	100.0%	100.0%	22,269,272

Sources: Number of new jobs: *Handbook of Small Business Data 1988*, Washington, D.C.: U.S. Small Business Administration, Office of Advocacy, 1988, pp. 203–224. Percentages, author's calculations based on: *Handbook of Small Business Data 1988*, Washington, D.C.: U.S. Small Business Administration, Office of Advocacy, 1988, pp. 203–224.

manufacturing jobs are not somehow stimulated in this country. As shown in Table 7.2, a total of 22.3 million new U.S. jobs were created between 1976 and 1986. Of these, 16.4 million (74 percent) came from the three lower-paying service industries discussed earlier. If this trend continues, eventually no less than 75 percent of all jobs will be in these sectors.

If the Big Three auto makers are willing to ignore and abandon a market of potentially 75 percent of the nongovernment work force, then in a world of free-market enterprise, they deserve whatever is their fate. The rest of the country need not follow them down this primrose path. A new small-car manufacturer can successfully compete in the United States.

UNION MEMBERS: THE LOGICAL ORGANIZERS

Union members are the most likely candidates to organize such an initiative. What organization knows more about the nuts and bolts of putting together a car than the United Auto Workers (UAW)? Starting a new auto company will require a bold vision of the future. However, first, it will require a realistic view of the present.

As part of this clear understanding of the present, auto workers (indeed, all manufacturing employees) are embroiled in a fight for their economic lives. Just as Japanese have capitalized on the low-cost labor throughout Asia, U.S. manufacturers have only begun to do the same in the Western Hemisphere. Already, Mexican *maquiladoras* are prospering near the border, where more than 1,500 assembly operations employ half a million Mexican citizens.

The North American Free Trade Zone will be a reality.[12] As the respective governments define the legal framework for the Free Trade Zone, these manufacturing facilities will spread further into the heartland of Mexico. The economics of the situation are irresistible. Including benefits, *maquiladora* employees earn $1.63 per hour. Assuming a 2,080-hour work year, this implies a total cost of $3,390 per year for a Mexican assembler vis-à-vis over $22,000 for his U.S. counterpart (see Table 7.1). Admittedly, over time there will be some upward pressure on Mexican wages, but there will be equivalent downward pressure on U.S. wages. This can only mean a lower standard of living in the United States.

This downward pressure has already begun. In the late 1980s, 70 percent of all union workers affected by collective bargaining accepted lower first-year wages under the terms of the new contract. In 1988, 91 percent of all manufacturing workers that were represented by unions had accepted one form of concession or another. Neither should the nonunion shops in Japanese auto transplants in the United States feel comforted. Nissan Mexicana is already investing $1 billion in a new plant and plans to bring nine of its Japanese suppliers with it. This trend promises to accelerate.

Second, union members must understand that they have lost the sympathy of the American consumer. Since 75 percent of the new jobs during the ten-year period ended 1986 pay less than the typical union manufacturing wage, even after the concessions, union members can scarcely expect to be viewed as hardship cases. When this disparity is combined with the well-publicized shoddy workmanship in the auto industry, it begins to look as if union workers may be more aptly described as greedy opportunists than deserving, patriotic Americans. In a nutshell, this is the perception of unions held by a great many people today.

This is not to suggest that this perception cannot be reversed. However, it will require a distinctly different vision of the future. In the future, unions must become better businesses. Businesses survive when they offer a needed service at a competitive price. Fifteen-dollar-an-hour assembly labor is not competitively priced and will, therefore, not be a service that is demanded indefinitely. On the other hand, a $4,000 to $5,000 automobile can enjoy significant market penetration.

Obviously, the technology, facilities, and manpower to organize a union car maker cannot be obtained costlessly. Individual union members may not have large amounts of discretionary funds. However, private and public pension funds hold roughly $2 trillion in financial assets alone. A significant proportion of these private and state and local government pension plans is negotiated through collective bargaining.[13] Some part of these funds should be available to beneficiaries to invest as they see fit.

Primarily, money managers control pension fund investments. By law, these money managers must live up to the standard of the prudent man rule of thumb, that is, they must act diligently, carefully, and prudently to make investments for the benefit of covered employees, their families, and dependents. However, almost half of the financial assets of pension funds are devoted to equities (mostly common stock). This high concentration exposes participants to considerable downside risk, especially as large U.S. corporations struggle to compete with foreign companies.

This is particularly disturbing since the fund participants have no voice either in the selection of these securities or in the operation of the firms that they represent. Pension funds hold almost 25 percent of all U.S. common stock (excluding mutual fund shares). Yet it is money managers, not fund participants, who may exercise an owner's voice as shareholders of the underlying firms.

It seems only reasonable that, with so much control currently in the hands of money managers, some portion of fund assets be allocated to purposes determined by the participants themselves. Sponsoring employers have already taken their option to terminate overfunded plans to capture the excess funding and direct it to other purposes. Why shouldn't the beneficiaries be given an equivalent right to invest in themselves and in products that they manufacture?

INNOVATION WITHIN THE BIG THREE AUTO MAKERS

Even with something less than state-of-the-art technology, the Big Three auto makers can improve both service and profits by having the imagination to differentiate their products from the Japanese versions. Perceptions of Japanese craftsmanship and dependability are already firmly entrenched in the minds of American customers. To overcome this, the quality of service offered must be head and shoulders above the competition. This service begins in the showroom and continues through the business office (including provision of insurance) and, later, the repair shop.

A fatal error that the auto industry has made in the United States is considering each of these phases as individual, free-standing, profit-making ventures. The manufacturer earns a markup over cost. The dealer earns more on the final sale to consumer, while his own finance office makes a spread on the financing. When the car must be serviced, parts and labor are marked up over actual cost.

This has been carried to such an extreme that purchasing replacement parts for a car can cost as much as three times the cost of the original auto. At the same time, the hourly rate charged for labor to repair the car can average from $28 to $35 per hour, even though the mechanic may earn a fraction of this rate. Instead of trying to gouge the consumer at every step along the way, a more visionary approach could win back the respect and patronage of Americans through carefully controlling every phase of the manufacture-purchase-repair cycle and earning a reasonable return on each phase.

The first critical element is manufacture. Here, the concept of labor compensation must be addressed. It is impossible to justify grossly exorbitant wages on the assembly line. At a minimum, the wage scale must be adjusted gradually up to double-digit hourly rates, and only then as more responsibility is assumed.

Union members must break from the past tradition of high wages based on favoritism and nepotism and move to a system of pay based on contribution and productivity. Like it or not, the United States is steadily evolving from a nation of high-paid, semiskilled labor to a country of lower-paid workers engaged in service industries, where the demand for higher-technological literacy is a fact of life. Within the manufacturing sector, a Mexican worker can be trained to operate the most sophisticated equipment for a fraction of U.S. union labor wages.

Of course, it is not necessary to go to Mexico to find employees willing to work in a manufacturing facility for less than union wages. In fact, union auto workers earning $15 to $20 per hour for relatively low-tech skills may be viewed by some observers as equivalent to winning a lottery, a fortunate turn of events predicated more on luck than on qualifications. In this environment, even white-collar workers feel the salary pinch and will increasingly opt for lower-priced cars. All of these pressures will inevitably shift more jobs offshore and cause even more robotics to be introduced.

Once manufactured, the final product should remain under the control of the car maker and be marketed in company-owned showrooms instead of private dealerships. This is roughly equivalent to the now common practice of retail service station ownership by major oil companies. Such an innovation should not be construed as manufacturers' disloyalty to dealers since these dealers already have the right to sell more than one line of cars. If a private dealer can increase profits by selling several models, he should do so. If a manufacturer can improve its profit picture by selling directly to the public, it should do so.

Even more fundamentally, the retail distribution of automobiles in the United States is often perceived as a series of consumer frauds. The dealer overcharges for a car that all too often needs numerous repairs that may or may not be covered by a warranty. Repairs that are not covered by warranty are too expensive. While the automobile is often the second largest investment that a family may make (after a primary residence), it loses as much as half its value in two to three years.

In any industry in which retail distribution tactics fall into such disrepute, manufacturers have an obligation to try to restore order and efficiency to the market. As important as the auto industry is, this responsibility cannot be ignored. Company-owned dealerships are one way to address these problems.

A primary function of these company-owned dealerships should be the systematic gathering of market research data through both structured and open-ended consumer surveys. One of the keys to Japanese success in the United States has been a tireless effort to identify and satisfy precise consumer preferences.

In addition, managers and other employees should be salaried, with customer interface being the responsibility of information specialists, not salespersons. Used-car salesmen are traditionally the least-respected members of the business community, with new-car salesmen following close behind. The reason for this appears to be linked to the distortion of the role of a salesperson. It should not be the job of this employee to close the deal, but instead to provide (and gather) information. If the car is well made and priced competitively, it will almost sell itself.

Why should a consumer be eager to cover the dealer's cost of a sales commission for a person who does little more than show the prospective buyer the car's interior and act as a middleman for dealership management? Such practices are as transparent as artificial price markups that are then marked back down and called "rebates" or as the $1,000 dealer-added rustproofing treatments on autos that are guaranteed against rust by the manufacturer.

A more honest approach would be for a salaried information specialist to be prepared to explain the details of the car's manufacture and why it is superior to the competition, if, in fact, it is. Unfortunately, during the 1980s, U.S. models were rarely better than the competition, which forced sales reps to resort to chicanery to move the inventory off the lot.

This leads to the next point. Captive finance companies and insurance firms are not being managed in an optimal fashion to enhance their respective auto makers' image. The financing arms should offer interest rates that are competitive with commercial banks and other lenders. The usual justification for higher rates has been that their clientele is riskier than a typical bank borrower. It is possible that the reverse could just as easily explain this phenomenon. High finance-company rates, often structured to provide a kickback to dealers, discourage less risky customers. Undue pressure to buy extended warranties on vehicles (that should have better warranties to begin with) is also a disincentive.

The key is to be more competitive at every stage of customer service. There is another tremendous opportunity to do so in the insurance area. Repair shops (connected with company-owned dealerships) can easily obtain auto parts for covered repairs directly from original parts suppliers, at the same cost that they are sold to the manufacturing division. In turn, savings on auto parts can be passed directly to the consumer, lowering both final repair bills and required insurance premiums. Of course, one required stipulation in a company-underwritten insurance policy would be that all repairs be performed in one of the specified company repair shops. However, from the customer's perspective, the relative inflexibility of this arrangement would be more than offset by substantial cost savings, guaranteed original factory parts, and increased accountability for the quality of repair work. Any serious customer complaints would go directly to manufacturing headquarters, which would exert pressure on managers of company-owned dealerships to satisfactorily resolve the situation.

With such innovations in production, distribution, financing, and insurance, persistent escalation in the cost of operating an American-made automobile can be reversed and substantial savings for the consumer realized. To win back lost market share, profit must be defined in a broader sense. Profit should not be defined simply as the markup on the finished product in isolation from the rest of the distribution system. Profits also should be measured in terms of gains in market share, sustained employment growth, and long-term viability. To the extent that these can be achieved, all of America will profit.

SAVING THE CITIES

Just as the combination of innovation and high-technology represents the hope of U.S. industry, the combination of inspired city management and high-technology can reverse the decline of some of the country's once most prosperous areas. City managers dismay that tax bases have deteriorated and that there is not enough money to pay for the services that are being demanded. Yet the sad truth is that urban development could not have been more poorly implemented if the stated objective had been to cause the demise of the central city.

Consider the sequence of events. As suburbia began to form just outside the city limits, its residents took advantage of lower property taxes and, in many cases, lower income taxes. How did the cities respond to this emigration? They continued to provide utility services at essentially the same rate that they were provided within the city. In other words, the new suburbanites received financial incentives to abandon the city. Of course, retail establishments followed them and the mall was born as an American phenomenon. In the process, the center city lost residents and businesses, in other words, lost economic vitality.

As outlying areas continue to sprawl, city systems have had to boost capacity. Whenever these expansions necessitate new construction to meet the higher demand or, at a minimum, greater maintenance costs because of the pressure on existing systems, usage rates typically increase for city and non-city residents alike. Thus, city residents pay higher rates even though they represent none of the increased service burden. Meanwhile, suburbanites pay only the incremental cost of providing service, avoiding the capital investment that would be required to establish separate suburban service.

Nowhere else in U.S. society is the cost of product development not absorbed by product users. When a new patented pharmaceutical preparation is offered to the public, its retail pricing reflects the scientific research and development that was required to bring the product to market. It is only after several years of such pricing that generic manufacturers may replicate the product at purely incremental cost. Using another example, U.S. defense contractors have the documented right to pass along developmental costs in the bidding and procurement processes. These cases are representative of common principles of business management.

Products and services must be priced to cover the cost of investment, direct or incremental cost, and a reasonable profit margin to provide development funds for product improvements. Outside city limits, the cost of city services should be higher than inside the city. Residents and businesses wishing to abandon the city should pay a premium to continue to receive city services. Surely, if municipalities ignore basic concepts of sound business management, the results are predictable — financial distress and bankruptcy.

Not only do municipalities tend to price themselves into extinction, they also literally pave the way to their own destruction. Extensive roadways and streets make commuting from the suburbs to the city fairly effortless. So, even when a certain number of employers remain within city limits, their employees have easy access to outlying areas, commuting sometimes long distances from home to work. Meanwhile, the city is left with air pollution from auto emissions, demands for convenient affordable parking facilities, and the costs of traffic control and road maintenance.

To illustrate, there are approximately 3.9 million miles of public roads, of which 2.8 million miles are under local (vis-à-vis state or federal) government control. Less than 22 percent of the total mileage of roads under local control is classified as urban, with the rest considered rural. Nevertheless, in fiscal 1988, municipalities spent almost 50 percent of the total local government outlays for highways and 84 percent of local expenditures for parking facilities.[14] These statistics show that cities bear more than their share of the cost of roads and road maintenance. What is less obvious, but equally true, is that these roads make it much easier for cities to be abandoned. Thus, cities tend to facilitate their own demise. At a minimum, commuters should be required to pay a toll to enter metropolitan areas in which they work but do not live, as is the case in New York City.

In fact, large cities bear more than their proportional burden for police protection, fire protection, parks and recreation, sewerage, solid waste, and utilities. The states shown in Table 7.3 represent almost 70 percent of the U.S. population.[15] Accordingly, the pattern of government finance in these states has important implications for the country as a whole.

On average, only 22 percent of the residents of these states live in cities with populations larger than 100,000, with the lowest percentage in New Jersey (10.2 percent) and the highest in New York (45.8 percent). However, large city expenditures in those categories noted above are almost always a higher percentage of total local government outlays than their populations should warrant. Still, these cities fall further and further behind as they attempt to salvage antiquated infrastructures with fewer and fewer resources.

TABLE 7.3
Large City Populations and Expenditures for Selected States, 1987–1988

State	Large cities population as a % of total (1)	Large cities expenditures as a % of total local government expenditures (2)					
		Police	Fire	Parks and Recreation	Sewer	Solid Waste	Utilities
Massachusetts	15.1%	34.2%	34.8%	34.4%	21.4%	30.2%	8.0%
New York	45.8	42.2	48.2	35.8	35.6	41.4	49.9
Illinois	30.2	53.5	31.5	10.8	25.9	59.1	24.2
Ohio	16.3	48.0	51.5	44.1	47.6	49.4	41.8
Texas	37.5	48.2	58.9	53.1	51.5	58.2	40.0
Colorado	33.9	48.9	45.1	45.0	39.6	43.8	41.1
Michigan	20.9	46.9	47.2	49.7	39.8	26.1	43.8
Florida	18.3	31.4	36.2	36.2	35.8	26.0	41.9
California	36.4	43.3	33.5	38.5	35.1	45.2	28.5
Kentucky	13.4	43.3	51.5	48.7	32.6	51.7	48.9
Wisconsin	16.3	42.7	54.4	30.8	26.8	45.1	50.7
Louisiana	22.8	31.0	43.8	47.0	37.4	42.0	42.9
New Jersey	10.2	33.8	38.3	19.9	16.2	28.1	32.8
Pennsylvania	20.0	44.0	49.7	36.6	21.0	43.0	22.9
Oregon	14.2	42.3	34.8	38.8	44.8	12.6	33.9
Missouri	21.9	49.0	44.5	43.1	38.2	59.0	47.0
Georgia	13.9	32.3	32.4	35.1	33.1	39.1	24.3
Washington	14.2	39.8	41.9	39.6	25.1	36.7	16.5

Notes: (1) the aggregate 1986 population of those cities of at least 100,000 residents as a percentage of total state population; (2) represents 60 percent of total expenditures by municipalities in the relevant category as a percentage of total local government expenditures for fiscal year 1987–1988. [In 1987, 41 percent of all U.S. municipal governments represented populations of 100,000 or more. In 1986, municipal governments of cities with at least 100,000 residents collected revenues and made expenditures totaling 62 percent of all municipal government revenues and expenditures, respectively. Local government expenditures include all those made by municipalities, counties, townships, and special districts.]

Sources: Author's calculations based on: *Government Finances in 1987–1988*. Washington, D.C.: U.S. Department of Commerce, Bureau of the Census, 1990, pp. 45–96; *Statistical Abstract of the United States*, 1989, 109th e. Washington, D.C.: U.S. Department of Commerce, Bureau of the Census, 1989.

As more well-to-do citizens move away, many of the service industries that cater to them follow. A good number of those individuals who are left find themselves unemployed and without access to transportation that they need to follow their former jobs to the suburbs. Inevitably, where there is wide-scale unemployment, there will be crime. The cycle then feeds on itself as crime encourages still others to leave and take even more jobs as they go. The U.S. inner city becomes the antithesis (opposite) of Singapore or Hong Kong, both cities where economic activity is concentrated in a relatively small area such that everyone can tap into the dynamic market forces at work. On the contrary, in the United States, it is more common to see cities suffering a steady population exodus and hemorrhaging from a steady flow of red ink.

One wonders why it was so difficult for city fathers to anticipate this scenario as, first, outlying residential areas were developed and, then, billions of dollars in public funds were expended to build the roads necessary to connect these now far-flung suburbs. Is it possible that purse strings held by real estate developers suggested a more compelling agenda for city commissioners, managers, and planners than the long-term viability of the cities with which they were charged?

Whatever is the explanation, the only way to reverse these trends is to address them economically. Higher city income taxes are not the solution because they only serve to penalize those who choose to remain in the city. Instead, the opposite form of incentives is necessary. Those who work in the city but do not reside there should be assessed appropriate user fees for city services. Those who neither work nor live in the central city, but tap into city-provided utilities and other services should pay a premium for them. If even half of those people that moved out of the central city in the last two decades could be encouraged to move back in, many large municipalities could probably stop the financial juggling act that they find themselves performing.[16]

Even these adjustments, however, will not cure all that ails the inner city. The infrastructure in most cities is, at best, old and under significant strain. Power supplies, water systems, and transportation facilities all have been modified over time to expand or upgrade service in patchwork fashion. This is somewhat analogous to modifying a Model T Ford by first adding a more powerful engine, next redesigning the wheels, then cutting down the roof and adding better shock absorbers for a smoother, more aerodynamic ride. While all of these measures help make the car a better Model T, it is still a Model T. On the other hand, an automobile built today, using the most advanced

technology available, has little resemblance to that first automotive wonder of mass production.

Likewise, a city built today, using the most advanced technology, would have little resemblance to those cities settled at the turn of the twentieth century. As a point of departure, it is readily apparent that constructing a city for maximum accessibility by automobiles is a mistake. To do so compromises both the environment (air and noise pollution) and the general quality of life.

Typically, the most valuable residential real estate in a metropolitan area is that which is relatively close to the central city, yet removed from heavy traffic congestion. A state-of-the-art city would be planned around people rather than automobiles. Clean, safe, and dependable mass transportation is feasible, but rarely seen in today's cities because of over-dependence on the auto. Further, in a city built from the ground up, solar and wind-driven alternative power sources can be more easily constructed on a large enough scale so as to make them more cost-effective. The new infrastructure for commerce and industry can be designed to be more environmentally compatible than would be possible with modifications of older systems. Fiber-optic telecommunications systems can make it possible to link residents directly to businesses, consumers to retailers, employees to employers. In short, more time could be spent creating and producing rather than in commuting.

Of course, this will require experimental cities to perfect the new city planning process. However, this is decidedly a more reasonable approach than continuing to pour billions of dollars into obsolete systems. Either way, the United States will eventually pay the price.

THE CHOICES

The United States may pay the price to become more productive and efficient by supporting from-the-ground-up experiments in new approaches to city life, entrepreneurship in product development and manufacture, and the proliferation of small firms. Even though this is an admittedly aggressive stance, it is the country's one best hope to avoid a continuing decline of living standards.

Truthfully, the United States is no longer the center of the world's economy. Instead, it is only one of several regions with substantial economic clout. Collectively, the country may decide to compete, that is, make an honest assessment of its strengths and weaknesses, and move boldly ahead. Alternatively, it may continue to use past approaches to current problems, stagnate and become the Model T of the world's

economy, continuing to putter along but never again quite getting up to speed.

There will be no global prosperity. And there will be no sustained regional prosperity in the United States unless Americans view the world as it is rather than as they would like it to be, avoid repeating past mistakes, and take full advantage of the opportunities to realize unprecedented levels of prosperity.

NOTES

1. In the United States, the Big Three automobile manufacturers are General Motors, Ford, and Chrysler.

2. The following fiscal 1991 deficits were estimated (*U.S. News and World Report*, 12-31-90; *USA Today*, 12-26-90):

New York	$ 1 billion
New Jersey	500 million
Pennsylvania	1 billion
Massachusetts	400 million
Virginia	2 billion
District of Columbia	200 million

3. In 1983 and 1989, for each of the following categories of employees, the percentages of those employees with strong positive assessments of senior management were as follows (Farnham, 1989):

	1983	1989
Managers	70%	50%
Professional staff	54%	40%
Hourly workers	42%	30%

4. The 50 states were ranked by descending order of 1989 per capita personal income (*Survey of Current Business*, August 1990). The ranked list was then divided into five groups of ten states each. Below the per capita income range is shown for each of the five groups. The percentage of new jobs generated in enterprises with less than 100 employees (simple average for the ten states) from 1976 through 1986 is also shown (*Handbook of Small Business Data 1988*).

Personal income range	% of new jobs in small firms
$18,927–$24,683	43.5%
$17,269–$18,824	48.0%
$15,779–$16,498	45.2%
$13,707–$15,702	35.6%
$11,724–$13,685	25.2%

5. From 1980 through 1989, aggregate gross fixed capital formation (GFCF) and gross national product (GNP) for the respective countries were as follows (*International Financial Statistics*, yearbook, 1990):

Country	GFCF (trillions)	GNP (trillions)
Japan	¥911.2	¥3,097.9
Germany	DM3.7	DM18.3
United States	$6.8	$39.0

6. At 12.5 percent, a four-year $10,000 loan requires a monthly payment of $265.80.

7. If the car averages 20 miles per gallon, the owner drives 10,000 miles a year, and gasoline costs $1.25 per gallon, annual gasoline expense amounts to $625 (or $52 per month). Purchasing a relatively inexpensive insurance policy at $600 a year adds another $50 per month.

8. Assuming that net earnings are 75 percent of the average annual earnings of $9,829, $614 remains as monthly bring-home pay. Reducing this by the $350 required to operate the auto, the remaining amount is $264.

9. In 1987, the distribution of after-tax income for one-half of all U.S. families was as follows (*A Marketeer's Guide to Discretionary Income*, 1989):

% of families	Annual after-tax earnings
30.2%	$ 7,628
10.4%	15,319
9.6%	19,095

10. With nonsupervisory retail trade employees representing 88.5 percent of the industry total, 11.5 percent must be considered supervisory. This is a ratio of 7.7 to 1.

11. The average American automobile production run is 225,000 units vis-à-vis 112,550 for the Japanese counterpart (Katayama, 1990).

12.   The North American Free Trade Zone is being discussed as a regional trade arrangement for the free flow of goods, services, and capital throughout the United States, Canada, and Mexico. Conceptually, it is similar to the Single European Market of the European Community.

13.   Of all civilian workers, 43 percent are covered by pension plans and 19 percent are represented by unions (*Statistical Abstract of the United States, 1989*).

14.   During fiscal 1988, municipal and total local government expenditures (by counties, municipalities, townships, and special districts) for highways and parking facilities were as follows (in millions of dollars) (*Government Finances in 1987–1988*, 1990):

	Municipalities	Total local
Highways	$10,732	$21,889
Parking facilities	662	785

15.   The 18 states in Table 7.3 had an aggregate population of 166.2 million in 1987, when the country's total population stood at 243.4 million (*Statistical Abstract of the United States, 1989*).

16.   From 1970 through 1986, the following selected cities lost substantial shares of their populations (in thousands) (*Statistical Abstract of the United States, 1989*):

	1986 population	16-year loss
Boston	574	67
Buffalo	325	138
New York	7,263	633
Chicago	3,010	359
Cincinnati	370	84
Detroit	1,086	428
Louisville	286	75
Milwaukee	605	112
New Orleans	554	39
Newark	316	66
Philadelphia	1,643	306
St. Louis	426	196
Atlanta	422	73
Seattle	486	45
Washington, D.C.	622	135

Bibliography

Adams, T. F. M., and Iwao Hoshii. *A Financial History of the New Japan.* Tokyo: Kodansha International Ltd., 1972.

Adomeit, Hannes. "Gorbachev and German Reunification: Revision of Thinking, Realignment of Power." *Problems of Communism*, 39 (July–August 1990). Washington, D.C.: U.S. Information Agency, pp. 1–23.

"American CEOs Rake in the Cash — and Worries to Match." *Business Week* (no. 3187), November 12, 1990, p. 22.

Baker, Stephen, Elizabeth Weiner, and Amy Borrus. "Mexico: A New Economic Era." *Business Week* (no. 3187), November 12, 1990, p. 102–10.

Bank of Japan. *Comparative Economic and Financial Statistics: Japan and Other Major Countries, 1988.* Tokyo: Bank of Japan, 1988.

"The Battleground of Chad." *Africa Report*, vol. 35, no. 4 (September–October 1990). New York: African-American Institute, p. 62.

Bell, Linda A. "Union Concessions in the 1980s." *Federal Reserve Bank of New York Quarterly Review.* New York: Federal Reserve Bank of New York, Summer 1989.

The Black Population in the United States: March 1988. Washington, D.C.: U.S. Department of Commerce. Bureau of the Census. November 1989.

Bouchet, Michael H., and Jonathan Hay. "The Rise of the Market-Based "Menu" Approach and Its Limitations." *Dealing with the Debt Crisis*, edited by Ishrat Husain and Ishac Diwan. Washington, D.C.: World Bank, 1989, pp. 146–59.

Bronte, Stephen. *Japanese Finance: Markets and Institutions.* London: Euromoney Publications, 1982.

Budget of the United States Government, Historical Tables, Fiscal Year 1990. Washington, D.C.: U.S. Government Printing Office, 1989.

Byrd, Robert C. "Examining American Assistance to Eastern Europe." *Harvard International Review*, vol. 13, no. 1 (Fall 1990). Cambridge, Mass.: Harvard International Relations Council, pp. 12–14.

"Can Islam, Democracy, and Modernization Co-exist?" *Africa Report*, vol. 35, no. 4 (September–October 1990). New York: African-American Institute, p. 9.

"Capital Market Financing for Developing Countries." *International Capital Markets: Developments and Prospects.* Washington, D.C.: International Monetary Fund, April 1990, pp. 26–43.

The Caribbean: Export Preferences and Performance. Washington, D.C.: World Bank, 1988.

"Change in Cross-Border Bank Claims on Developing Countries and Areas 1983 — Third Quarter 1988." *International Capital Markets: Developments and Prospects.* Washington, D.C.: International Monetary Fund, April 1989, p. 86.

"Change in Cross-Border Claims on Developing Countries and Areas, 1983 — Third Quarter 1989." *International Capital Markets: Developments and Prospects.* Washington, D.C.: International Monetary Fund, April 1990, p. 90.

China, External Trade and Capital. Washington, D.C.: World Bank, 1989.

China, Finance and Investment. Washington, D.C.: World Bank, 1988.

Curry, David, and Geoffrey Dicks. "Recession Will Start to Fade in New Year." *Sunday Times*, London, October 28, 1990, p. 4.3.

"Debt and Debt Service Reduction in Commercial Bank Agreements, 1987–89." *International Capital Markets: Developments and Prospects.* Washington, D.C.: International Monetary Fund, April 1990, pp. 104–6.

Dentzer, Susan, Jeff Trumble, and Bruce B. Auster. "The Soviet Economy in Shambles." *U.S. News and World Report*, vol. 107, no. 20, November 20, 1989,pp. 25–39.

Department of Trade and Industry and the Central office of Information. *Europe 1992: The Facts.* London, United Kingdom, February 1989.

Economic and Social Commission for Asia and the Pacific. *Foreign Trade Statistics of Asia and the Pacific.* New York: United Nations, 1989.

Fallows, James. "Japan's Secret Weapon." *U.S. News and World Report*, vol. 107, no. 25 (December 25, 1989), p. 46.

Farnham, Alan. "The Trust Gap." *Fortune*, December 4, 1989, pp. 56–78.

Financial Solidarity for Development: Development Assistance from OPEC Members and Institutions to Other Developing Countries: 1982–1986: 1988 Supplement. New York: United Nations, 1988.

"German Bank's Lending to Developing Countries, 1985 — Third Quarter 1988." *International Capital Markets: Developments and Prospects.* Washington, D.C.: International Monetary Fund, April 1989, p. 122.

Glover-James, Ian Grice, and Andrew Grice. "PM Mocks Unity as Euro Farm Talks Fail." *Sunday Times,* London, October 28, 1990, p. 1.2.

Government Finances in 1987–1988. Washington, D.C.: U.S. Department of Commerce, Bureau of the Census, GF-88-5, January 1990.

Grice, Andrew. "Sorry, the Lady's Not Ready to Tie EC Knots." *Sunday Times,* London, October 18, 1990, p. 3.2.

Grilli, Vittorio. "Europe 1992: Issues and Prospects for the Financial Markets." *Economic Policy: A European Forum.* New York: Press Syndicate of the University of Cambridge, October 1989, pp. 388–411.

Hammes, Sara. "An Insider's Guide to Seven Cities." *Fortune: Asia: Mega-Market of the 1990s,* vol. 122, no. 8 (Special Issue, Fall 1990), pp. 69–78.

Handbook of International Trade and Development Statistics 1988. New York: United Nations, 1988.

Handbook of Small Business Data 1988. Washington, D.C.: Small Business Data Base, U.S. Small Business Administration, Office of Advocacy, November 1988.

Hewett, Ed. A. *Reforming the Soviet Economy: Equality vs. Efficiency.* Washington, D.C.: Brookings Institution, 1988.

Holstein, William J., David Woodruff, and Amy Borrus. "Is Free Trade With Mexico Good or Bad for the U.S.?" *Business Week* (no. 3187), November 12, 1990, pp. 112–13.

Horisaka, Kotaro. "Japanese Banks and the Latin American Debt Problems." Unpublished manuscript, Sophia University, Tokyo, Japan, 1989.

Huat, Tan Chwee. *Financial Institutions in Singapore.* Singapore: Singapore University Press, 1981.

Huizinga, Harry. "The Commercial Bank Claims on Developing Countries: How have Banks Been Affected?" *Dealing with the Debt Crisis,* edited by Ishrat Husain and Ishac Diwan. Washington, D.C.: World Bank, 1989, pp. 129–43.

"International Bond Issues by Developing Countries, 1983–88." *International Capital Markets: Developments and Prospects.* Washington, D.C.: International Monetary Fund, April 1989, p. 87.

"International Bond Issues by Developing Countries, 1983–89." *International Capital Markets: Developments and Prospects.* Washington, D.C.: International Monetary Fund, April 1990, p. 92.

International Financial Statistics, vol. 43, no. 5. Washington, D.C.: International Monetary Fund, May 1990.

International Financial Statistics, vol. 43, yearbook. Washington, D.C.: International Monetary Fund, 1990.

Japan Economic Almanac. 1989.

Katayama, Ryuji. "From Dream to Reality." *Business Tokyo,* vol. 4, no. 12 (December 1990), pp. 30–35.

Kessides, Christine, Timothy King, Mario Nuti, and Catherine Sokil, eds. *Financial Reform in Socialist Economies.* Washington, D.C.: World Bank, 1989.

Lawday, David. "A Question Mark Again: Unexpected Obstacles Are Appearing in the Road to European Unity." *U.S. News and World Report,* October 15, 1990, pp. 61–64.

Lawday, David, and Alexander Stille. "Arrivederci, Italia? The Economic Gap Between North and South Divides Friends, Romans, and Countrymen." *U.S. News and World Report* (vol. 109, no. 19), November 12, 1990, pp. 46–50.

Lawrence, Robert Z., and Charles L. Schultze, eds. *Barriers to European Growth: A Transatlantic View.* Washington, D.C.: Brookings Institution, 1987.

Levey, Judith S., and Agnes Greenhall, eds. *The Concise Columbia Encyclopedia.* New York: Avon Books/Columbia University Press, 1983.

Lone, Salim. "Challenging Conditionality." *Africa Report,* vol. 35, no. 4 (September–October 1990). New York: African-American Institute, pp. 31–35.

A Marketer's Guide to Discretionary Income. Washington, D.C.: Bureau of the Census of the U.S. Department of Commerce and Conference Board of the Consumer Research Center, November 1989.

Mather, Ian. "Kremlin Still the Foe, Says Plan for NATO." *European,* London (no. 0024), October 19–21, 1990, p. 1.

Mather, Ian, and Chris Endean. "Britain Railroaded by the Single Currency Express." *European,* London (no. 0026), November 2–4, 1990, p. 4.

Meldrum, Andrew. "The Coup That Wasn't." *Africa Report,* vol. 35, no. 4 (September–October 1990). New York: African-American Institute, pp. 19–22.

Mills, Tony. "Genscher Gives Hurd a Taste of Germany Unity." *Sunday Times,* London, October 28, 1990, p. 1.16.

Morna, Colleen Lowe. "Nyerere's Turnabout." *Africa Report,* vol. 35, no. 4 (September–October 1990). New York: African-American Institute, pp. 23–25.

Morrison, Charles E., ed. *Japan, China, and the Newly Industrialized Economies of Asia: Discussion and Papers from a Symposium Held in Atlanta, Georgia.* Honolulu, Hawaii: East-West Center, October 1989.

Nabie, Isata, and John Prendergast. "A Land Divided." *Africa Report,* vol. 35, no. 4 (September–October 1990). New York: African-American Institute, pp. 58–61.

Nakayama, Taro. "Japan's Stance in Eastern Europe." *Harvard International Review,* vol. 13, no. 1 (Fall 1990). Cambridge, Mass.: Harvard International Relations Council, pp. 15-16, 60.

Naser, Sylvia. "It's Gloves-Off Time, America Undergoes an Industrial Revolution." *U.S. News and World Report* (vol. 107, no. 25), December 25, 1989, pp. 40–42.

National Trade Estimate Report on Foreign Trade Barriers. Washington, D.C.: Office of the United States Trade Representative, 1989.

"Off the Hook." *World Trade* (October/November 1990), Irvine, Calif.: Taipan Press, p. 18.

"Our Oil and the Future." *African Concord* (vol. 5, no. 24), October 15, 1990. Lagos, Nigeria: African Concord, Ltd., pp. 31–34.

"Political Pointers — Mauritania." *Africa Report,* vol. 35, no. 4, (September–October 1990). New York: African-American Institute, p. 7.

Rand McNally World Atlas. Chicago: Rand McNally, 1986.

Richman, Louis S. "How America Can Triumph." *Fortune* (vol. 120, no. 15), December 18, 1989, pp. 52–66.

Saporito, Bill. "Retailing's Winners and Losers." *Fortune* (vol. 120, no. 15), December 18, 1989, pp. 69–78.

Shields, Todd. "Lawyers vs. the Law." *Africa Report,* vol. 35, no. 4 (September–October 1990). New York: African-American Institute, pp. 13–18.

Skully, Michael T., ed. *Financial Institutions and Markets in the Far East: A Study of China, Hong Kong, Japan, South Korea, and Taiwan.* New York: St. Martin's Press, 1982.

____. *Financial Institutions and Markets in Southeast Asia: A Study of Brunei, Indonesia, Malaysia, Philippines, Singapore, and Thailand.* London: Macmillan Press Ltd., 1984.

Smolowe, Jill. "There Goes the Bloc." *Time* (vol. 134, no. 19), November 6, 1989, pp. 48–51.

Statistical Abstract of the United States, 1989, 109th ed. Washington, D.C.: U.S. Department of Commerce, Bureau of the Census, 1989.

Sub-Saharan Africa: From Crisis to Sustainable Growth. Washington, D.C.: World Bank, 1989.

Survey of Current Business, vol. 70, no. 8 (August 1990). United States Department of Commerce, Bureau of Economic Analysis.

Tan, Augustine H. H., and Basant Kapur. *Pacific Growth and Financial Interdependence*. North Sydney, Australia: Allen and Unwin, 1986.

Taylor, Alex, III. "Caution: Bumps Ahead at Ford." *Fortune* (vol. 120, no. 15) December 18, 1989, pp. 93–96.

Taylor, Ronald. "Eastern Europe: The World's Greatest Polluter." *Europe*, no. 300 (October 1990), pp. 17–19.

"Terms and Conditions of Bank Debt Restructurings and Financial Packages, 1987–89." *International Capital Markets: Developments and Prospects*. Washington, D.C.: International Monetary Fund, April 1990, pp. 93–98.

Tovias, Alfred. *The European Communities' Single Market: The Challenge of 1992 for Sub-Saharan Africa*. Washington, D.C.: World Bank, 1990.

Troiano, Peter. "The Latest in Luxury: Premium Japanese Autos." *Economic World* (November 1990), pp. 14–15. New York: Economic Salon.

Turner, John A., and Daniel J. Beller, eds. *Trends in Pensions*. Washington, D.C.: U.S. Department of Labor, Pension and Welfare Benefits Administration, 1989.

Ungeheuer, Frederick. "A Chasm of Misery." *Time* (vol. 134, no. 19), November 6, 1989, pp. 64–66.

United States Trade: Performance in 1988. Washington, D.C.: U.S. Department of Commerce, International Trade Administration, September 1989.

USA Today, various issues.

Viner, Aron. *Inside Japanese Financial Markets*. Homewood, Ill.: Dow Jones-Irwin, 1988.

Washington Post, various issues.

World Bank. *World Development Report, 1989*. New York: Oxford University Press, 1989.

World Bank Atlas 1988. Washington, D.C.: World Bank, 1988.

World Bank Atlas 1989. Washington, D.C.: World Bank, 1989.

World Debt Tables: External Debt of Developing Countries, 1988–89 ed., vol. 1. Washington, D.C.: World Bank, 1988.

World Debt Tables, 1989–90: External Debt of Developing Countries, vol. 1. Washington, D.C.: World Bank, 1989.

World Economic Outlook. Washington, D.C.: International Monetary Fund, May 1990.

World Military Expenditures and Arms Transfers 1988. Washington, D.C.: United States Arms Control and Disarmament Agency, 1988.

Index

About the Author

Hazel J. Johnson is currently a professor in the School of Business, Department of Economics and Finance, University of Louisville, and was formerly a professor at Georgetown University in Washington, D.C. An expert in the finance field, she is working on two future books, *Financial Institutions and Markets: A Global Perspective* and *Foundations of Capital Budgeting.*